Essays for All

Making Essay Writing Easy

READERS CHOICE

New Delhi - 110002

Essays for All

Making Essay Writing Easy

Kavita Nagpal

READERS CHOICE
New Delhi - 110002

Essays for All

Making Essay Writing Easy

ISBN 978-81-922292-2-5

Published by:

Readers Choice

103, 4787/23, Ansari Road,
Daryaganj, New Delhi - 110002
Ph: 9654444181

Laser typesetting by: Naissance Books, New Delhi.
Printed at: Navprabhat Printing Press, Delhi

Essays for All

Making Essay Writing Easy

READERS CHOICE
(Quality Books for All)
New Delhi-110002

Published by:
Readers Choice

Essays for All

Making Essay Writing Easy

Kavita Nagpal

READERS CHOICE

(Quality Books for All)

New Delhi-110002

Published by:

Readers Choice

101, 4787/23, Ansari Road,
Daryaganj, New Delhi-110002,
Ph.: 23262179, 9311037185
E-mail: readerschoicepublications@gmail.com

Essays for All

Making Essay Writing Easy

ISBN 978-81-922292-2-5

Price : 125/-

Lasertypesetting by: Naissance Books, New Delhi.
Printed at: Navprabhat Printing Press, Delhi.

Preface

Students are required to write essay on several subjects in different academic and career situations. Talking about the significance of essay, we can say that it is a device for the assessment of student's research and writing skills, his/her critical approach along with word limit management.

Essay is said to be very important in one's educational life because it is the first and the foremost kind of writing that students are needed to write by their schools, or we can say that essay is the first step to enter into the world of writing. This is the reason why essay has a central and the most important position which no other form of writing can overpower.

Though essay writing is not very easy and simple; it needs practice and the students have to learn essay writing rules and about the collection of material. A student must have a critical and analytical mind that is keen to research on any specified essay topic.

Schooling is the first step of a person's educational life. Essays are needed by the teachers to test student's writing and searching skills which reflects their critical and analytical thinking. There are so many types of essays; it can be admission essay, an argumentative essay, critical essay and so on. Pre-school essays are not very demanding but secondary school students must learn about the format of essay and how to comment on or evaluate any specific topic. An essay is not only judged apparently on its structure but it is evaluated throughout its language, writing style and compliance to the topic.

The present book not brings a collection of essays but also highlights the procedure of writing essays and the ways students can improve their essay writing skills.

-Author

Contents

1

What is an Essay?

An **essay** is a piece of writing which is often written from an author's personal point of view. Essays can consist of a number of elements, including: literary criticism, political manifestos, learned arguments, observations of daily life, recollections, and reflections of the author. The definition of an essay is vague, overlapping with those of an article and a short story.

Types of Essays

Admission Essay

Essays are used to learn more about your reasons for applying to the course, university or company and your ability to benefit from and contribute to it. Your answers will let you state your case more efficiently than other sections of the application, and provide the evaluator with better insight about you and how you differ from the other applicants. In marginal cases, the essays are used to decide whether an applicant will be selected. The purpose of the admissions essay is to convey a sense of your unique character to the admissions committee. The essay also demonstrates your writing skills as well as your ability to organize your thoughts coherently.

Argumentative Essay

The function of an argumentative essay is to show that your assertion (opinion, theory, hypothesis) about some phenomenon or phenomena is correct or more truthful than others. The art of argumentation is not an easy skill to acquire. Many people might think that if one simply has an opinion, one can argue it successfully, and these folks are always surprised when others don't agree with them because their logic seems so correct.

Argumentative writing is the act of forming reasons, making inductions, drawing conclusions, and applying them to the case in discussion; the operation of inferring propositions, not known or admitted as true, from facts or principles known, admitted, or proved to be true. It clearly explains the process of your reasoning from the known or assumed to the unknown.

Without doing this you do not have an argument, you have only an assertion, an essay that is just your unsubstantiated opinion.

Cause and Effect Essay

Cause and effect essays are concerned with why things happen (causes) and what happens as a result (effects). Cause and effect is a common method of organizing and discussing ideas.

Classification Essay

In a classification essay, a writer organizes, or sorts, things into categories.

Comparison Essay

To write a comparison or contrast essay that is easy to follow, first decide what the similarities or differences are by writing lists on scrap paper. Which are more significant, the similarities or the differences? Plan to discuss the less significant first, followed by the more significant. It is much easier to discuss only the similarities or only the differences, but you can also do both.

Then for organizing your essay, choose one of the plans described below whichever best fits your list. Finally, this is important, what main point (thesis) might you make in the essay about the two people/things being compared? Do not begin writing until you have a point that the similarities or differences you want to use help to prove. Your point should help shape the rest of what you say: For example, if you see that one of your similarities or differences is unrelated to the point, throw it out and think of one that is related. Or revise your point. Be sure this main point is clearly and prominently expressed somewhere in the essay.

Critical Essay

The word "critical" has positive as well as negative meanings. You can write a critical essay that agrees entirely with the reading. The word "critical" describes your attitude when you read the article. This attitude is best described as "detached evaluation," meaning that you weigh the coherence of the reading, the completeness of its data, and so on, before you accept or reject it.

Deductive Essay

Deductive essays are an important factor in evaluating the

knowledge level of students in many courses. Deductive reasoning is based on the concept that given as set of circumstances or clues (premises), one can draw a reasonable assumption as to the state of the situation. More simply, a person can solve a puzzle or identify a person if given enough information.

Definition Essay

A definition essay is writing that explains what a term means. Some terms have definite, concrete meanings, such as glass, book, or tree. Terms such as honesty, honour, or love are abstract and depend more on a person's point of view.

Exploratory Essay

The concept of an exploratory essay is that you start without an end in mind. You don't necessarily know how you feel about a subject or what you want to say about the subject, you allow the research and your own direction to determine the outcome. This is writing to learn rather than writing to prove what you know. The exploratory essay builds on the inquiry essay by having you look at and contribute to a range of arguments rather than just one at a time. Whereas the inquiry essay introduced you to a debate by looking at one argument a time, the exploratory essay asks you to widen your vision to the whole conversation.

Expository Essay

The purpose of an expository essay is to present, completely and fairly, other people's views or to report about an event or a situation. Expository writing, or exposition, presents a subject in detail, apart from criticism, argument, or development; i.e., the writer elucidates a subject by analysing it. Such writing is discourse designed to convey information or explain what is difficult to understand. Exposition usually proceeds by the orderly analysis of parts and the use of familiar illustrations or analogies.

Informal Essay

The informal essay is written mainly for enjoyment. This is not to say that it cannot be informative or persuasive; however, it is less a formal statement than a relaxed expression of opinion, observation, humour or pleasure. A good informal essay has a relaxed style but retains a strong structure, though that structure may be less rigid than in a formal paper.

Narrative Essay

As a mode of expository writing, the narrative approach, more than any other, offers writers a chance to think and write about themselves. We all have experiences lodged in our memories, which are worthy of sharing with readers. Yet sometimes they are so fused with other memories that a lot of the time spent in writing narrative is in the prewriting stage.

Personal Essay

The overall application package will represent who "you" are to people whom you will most likely not know personally. The written expression of your qualities as an applicant will often be a very important way for committee members to get to know why you are an acceptable candidate for their programme.

Thus, it is essential to take great care in preparing this part of your application. Because graduate schools make important selection decisions that are partly based on what you say in this essay, the writing of it can be an intimidating prospect.

Persuasive Essay

Persuasive writing, also known as the argument essay, utilizes logic and reason to show that one idea is more legitimate than another idea. It attempts to persuade a reader to adopt a certain point of view or to take a particular action. The argument must always use sound reasoning and solid evidence by stating facts, giving logical reasons, using examples, and quoting experts.

Research Essay

Take care in selecting your thesis. This is really a type of persuasive essay, but you don't want to be stuck either just repeating someone else's opinion, or citing all the same sources. Try to come up with an original thesis or take an aspect of someone's thesis and develop it. You can also take a thesis and "transplant" it into different circumstances.

For example, use the past trends of globalization and to argue about its role of in the present day Indian economy and its future prospects, or take a study done on the role played by media in the past and showcase its present status. An original thesis is the best start you can make to get a high grade in a research essay.

Scholarship Essay

Scholarship essays vary dramatically in subject. However, most of them require a recounting of personal experience.

These tips will be more helpful for writing personal essays, like for the Scholarship, than for writing academic essays.

Parts of an Essay

Introduction Paragraph

What is an introduction paragraph?

The introduction paragraph is the first paragraph of your essay.

What does it do?

It introduces the main idea of your essay. A good opening paragraph captures the interest of your reader and tells why your topic is important.

How to write one?

1. Write the thesis statement. The main idea of the essay is stated in a single sentence called the thesis statement. You must limit your entire essay to the topic you have introduced in your thesis statement.

2. Provide some background information about your topic. You can use interesting facts, quotations, or definitions of important terms you will use later in the essay.

Example: Democracy without discipline is a body without soul. If there is no discipline in the country, democracy will degenerate into a monocracy i.e., a Government by a unruly crowd. In fact, in Greek 'Demos' means crowd. The word 'curacy' is from the Greek word 'Krait' or 'Cratos' which means power.

Supporting Paragraphs

What are supporting paragraphs?

Supporting paragraphs make up the main body of your essay.

What do they do?

They develop the main idea of your essay.

How to write them?

1. List the points that develop the main idea of your essay.
2. Place each supporting point in its own paragraph.
3. Develop each supporting point with facts, details, and examples.

To connect your supporting paragraphs, you should use special transition words. Transition words link your paragraphs together and make your essay easier to read. Use them at the beginning and end of your paragraphs.

Examples of transition words that can help you to link your paragraphs together:

For listing different points

- First
- Second
- Third

For counter examples

- However
- Even though
- On the other hand
- Nevertheless

For additional ideas

- Another
- In addition to
- Related to

- Furthermore
- Also

To show cause and effect

- Therefore
- Thus
- As a result of
- Consequently

Like all good paragraphs, each supporting paragraph should have a topic sentence, supporting sentences, and a summary sentence.

Summary Paragraph

What is a summary paragraph?

The summary paragraph comes at the end of your essay after you have finished developing your ideas. The summary paragraph is often called a 'conclusion.'

What does it do?

It summarizes or restates the main idea of the essay. You want to leave the reader with a sense that your essay is complete.

How to write one?

1. Restate the strongest points of your essay that support your main idea.
2. Conclude your essay by restating the main idea in different words.
3. Give your personal opinion or suggest a plan for action.

Example: Therefore, it is the foremost duty of all citizens of India to remain united and disciplined, to defeat the designs of foreign powers to destroy the unity of India and the democratic set-up of our country. By discipline and unity alone can democracy prosper in our country, and we remain free.

Ten Easy Steps to Write a Good Essay

Learning how to write an essay can be a maddening, exasperating process, but it doesn't have to be. If you know the steps and understand what to do, writing can be easy and even fun. Below are brief summaries of each of the ten steps to writing an essay.

1. *Research:* Begin the essay writing process by researching your topic, making yourself an expert. Utilize the internet, the academic databases, and the library. Take notes and immerse yourself in the words of great thinkers.

2. *Analysis:* Now that you have a good knowledge base, start analysing the arguments of the essays you're reading. Clearly define the claims, write out the reasons, the evidence. Look for weaknesses of logic, and also strengths. Learning how to write an essay begins by learning how to analyse essays written by others.

3. *Brainstorming:* Your essay will require insight of your own, genuine essay-writing brilliance. Ask yourself a dozen questions and answer them. Meditate with a pen in your hand. Take walks and think and think until you come up with original insights to write about.

4. *Thesis*: Pick your best idea and pin it down in a clear assertion that you can write your entire essay around. Your thesis is your main point, summed up in a concise sentence that lets the reader know where you're going, and why. It's practically impossible to write a good essay without a clear thesis.

5. *Outline*: Sketch out your essay before straightway writing it out. Use one-line sentences to describe paragraphs, and bullet points to describe what each paragraph will contain. Play with the essay's order. Map out the structure of your argument, and make sure each paragraph is unified.

6. *Introduction*: Now sit down and write the essay. The introduction should grab the reader's attention, set-up the issue, and lead in to your thesis. Your intro is merely a buildup of the issue, a stage of bringing your reader into the essay's argument.

   Note: The title and first paragraph are probably the most important elements in your essay. This is an essay-writing point that doesn't always sink in within the context of the classroom. In the first paragraph you either hook the reader's interest or lose it. Of course your teacher, who's getting paid to teach you how to write an essay, will read the essay you've written regardless, but in the real world, readers make up their minds about whether or not to read your essay by glancing at the title alone.

7. *Paragraphs*: Each individual paragraph should be focused on a single idea that supports your thesis. Begin paragraphs with topic sentences, support assertions with evidence, and expound your ideas in the clearest, most sensible way you can. Speak to your reader as if he or she were sitting in front of you. In other words, instead of writing the essay, try talking the essay.

8. *Conclusion*: Gracefully exit your essay by making a quick wrap-up sentence, and then end on some memorable thought, perhaps a quotation, or an interesting twist of logic, or some call to action. Is there something you want the reader to walk away and do? Let him or her know exactly what.

9. *MLA Style*: Format your essay according to the correct guidelines for citation. All borrowed ideas and quotations should be correctly cited in the body of your text, followed up with a Works Cited (references) page listing the details of your sources.

10. *Language:* You're not done writing your essay until you've polished your language by correcting the grammar, making sentences flow, incorporating rhythm, emphasis, adjusting the formality, giving it a level-headed tone, and making other intuitive edits. Proofread until it reads just how you want it to sound. Writing an essay can be tedious, but you don't want to bungle the hours of conceptual work you've put into writing your essay by leaving a few sloppy misspellings and poorly worded phrases.

Using Quotations in Essays

If you want to make an impact on your reader, you can draw on the potential of quotations. The effective use of quotations augments the power of your arguments and makes your essays more interesting.

But there is need for caution! Are you convinced that the quotation you have chosen is helping your essay and not hurting it? Here is a checklist to ensure that you are doing the right thing:

What is this Quotation Doing in this Essay?

Let us begin at the beginning. You have a chosen a quotation for your essay. But, why that specific quotation?

A good quotation should do one or more of the following:

- make an opening impact on the reader
- build credibility for your essay
- add humour

- make the essay more interesting
- close the essay with a point to ponder upon.

If the quotation does not meet a few of these objectives, then it is of little value. Merely stuffing a quotation into your essay can do more harm than good.

Your Essay is your Mouthpiece

Should the quotation speak for the essay or should the essay speak for the quotation? Quotations should add impact to the essay and not steal the show. If your quotation has more punch than your essay, then something is seriously wrong. Your essay should be able to stand on its own legs; the quotation should merely make this stand stronger.

How Many Quotations should you use in your Essay?

Using too many quotations is like having several people shouting hoarse on your behalf. This will drown your voice. Refrain from overcrowding your essay with words of wisdom from famous people. You own the essay, so make sure that you are heard.

Are there any expected standards for using quotations in an essay? Yes, there are. The most important one is that you should not give the impression of being the author of the quotation. That would amount to plagiarism. Here are a set of rules to clearly distinguish your writing from the quotation:

- Sometimes, you describe the quotation in your own words before using it. In this case, you should use a colon (:) to indicate the beginning of the quotation. Then begin the quotation with a quotation mark ("). After you have completed the quotation, close it with a quotation mark ("). Here is an example:

Sir Winston Churchill made a witty remark on the attitude of a pessimist: "A pessimist sees the difficulty in every opportunity; an optimist sees the opportunity in every difficulty."

- Sometimes the sentence in which the quotation is embedded does not describe the quotation, but merely introduces it. In this case, do away with the colon. Simply use the quotation marks. Here is an example:

  Mahatma Gandhi once said "It is better to be violent, if there is violence in our hearts, than to put on the cloak of nonviolence to cover impotence."

- As far as possible, you should mention the author and the source of the quotation. For instance:

  In Shakespeare's play *As You Like It*, Touchstone says to Audrey in the Forest of Arden "The fool doth think he is wise, but the wise man knows himself to be a fool." (Act V, Scene I).

- Ensure that the source of your quotation is authentic. Also, verify the author of your quotation. You can do so by looking up the quotation on authoritative Web sites, such as this one. But for formal writing, do not rely on just one Web site.

An essay can seem quite jarring if the quotation does not blend in. The quotation should naturally fit into your essay. No one is interested in reading quotation-stuffed essays.

Here are some good tips on blending in your quotations:

- You can begin your essay with a quotation that sets off the basic idea of the essay. This can have a lasting impact on your reader. In the introductory paragraph of your essay, you can comment on the quotation if you like. In any case, do ensure that the relevance of the quotation is communicated well.

- Your choice of phrases and adjectives can significantly boost the impact of the quotation in your essay. Do not go with monotonous phrases like:

  "Jawaharlal Nehru once said..."

  If your essay merits the use of powerful speech, consider using emphatic expressions like:

  "Jawaharlal Nehru rocked the nation by saying ..."

Long Quotations

It is usually better to have short and crisp quotations in your essay. However, if you are convinced that a particular long quotation is more effective, make sure that you follow the necessary rules.

When is it Appropriate to use Long Quotations in Your Essay?

It is your judgement call. Let me explain. Long quotations must be used sparingly as they tend to weigh down the reader. However, there are times when your essay has more impact with a longer quotation. If you have decided to use a long quotation, consider paraphrasing, as it usually works better. But, there is a flip side to paraphrasing too. Instead of the paraphrase, if you use a direct quotation, you will avoid misrepresentation. As you can see, the decision of using a long quotation is not trivial. Once again, it is your judgement call.

Punctuating Long Quotes

Long quotations should be set off as block quotations. Formatting block quotations should be as per the guidelines that you might have been provided. If there are no specific guidelines, you can follow the usual standard — if a quotation is more than three lines long, you block it. Blocking implies indenting it about half an inch on the left.

Often, setting up a long quotation is warranted. Writing a brief introduction displays your understanding of the subject. In other cases, you might need to provide a complete analysis of the quotation. In this case, it is best to state the quotation and follow it with the analysis, rather than the other way around.

Using Cute Quotes

Some students choose a cute quotation first, and then try to plug it into their essay. As a consequence, such quotations drag the reader away from the essay.

Quoting Poetry

Quoting a verse from a poem can add a lot of charm to your essay. If you are quoting from poetry, keep in mind that:

A small extract of a poem, say about two lines long, requires the use of slash marks (/) to indicate line breaks. Here is an example:

Vikram Seth has aptly described loneliness as "All you who sleep tonight / Far from the ones you love, / No hand to left or right / And emptiness above -."

If you use a single line extract of a poem, punctuate it like any other short quotation without the slashes. Quotation marks are required at the beginning and at the end of the extract. However, if your quotation is more than three lines of poetry, it is advisable to treat it like you would have treated a long quotation from prose. In this case, you should use the block quote format.

Does Your Reader Understand the Quotation?

Do you use quotations in your essays? Surely you follow the expected standards. But, that may not be enough. Having followed all the standards and punctuation, you must ask the critical question: "Do readers understand the quotation and its relevance to my essay?"

If the reader is re-reading a quotation, just to understand it, then you are in trouble. So when you choose a quotation for your essay, ask yourself the following questions:

- Is this too convoluted for my reader?
- Does this match the tastes of my audience?
- Is the grammar and vocabulary in this quotation understandable?

How to Use Transition Words and Phrases in an Essay?

Transition words and phrases are vital to the success of any essay. They are the bread and butter of writing. They are the glue that holds all essays together. Think of bricks building a house without mortar.

Lack of mortar would cause the house to fall apart without it. Transitions hold the same importance. We need these words and phrases to join sentences and thoughts together in a coherent fashion.

Here are a few tips on how and when to use transition words and phrases:

- Always use a transition phrase at the beginning of a new body paragraph
- Always use a transition word in between thoughts within a paragraph

- Never use a transition word to begin an essay
- Never use a transition word to begin a paragraph (but you can sometimes use a transition phrase at the start of a new body paragraph)

Here are some commonly used transition words and phrases:

- Consequently
- Therefore
- Because of
- As a result
- Rather
- Nonetheless
- Nevertheless
- Notwithstanding
- Furthermore
- In addition to
- Also

Transitions bring ideas together. They are leaving one thought and entering a new one. If you think of these words as ending the old and opening the new, it will help you organize your thoughts and your essays.

As another little tip from the inside, transition words are excellent cues on standardised tests. They often tell you what will be coming next (either positive or negative), and indicate a change. Furthermore, they are great words to stick into essays in high school and college. Teachers look for these words, as they indicate structure within an essay. As they are necessary to the continuity (and coherence) of an essay, they will demonstrate a firm grasp of a topic. If you use these words, then you know you have structured a strong essay, as you are building on an issue or are comparing two different issues well.

Things to Avoid While Writing an Essay

Essay writing is easy if you know the basic points of essay writing. If you want to know how to write a comparative essay then you need to select a topic, which is different from the others, or you can say a unique topic. Even if you really want to learn essay writing, which has perfect content, then there are certain things, which you must need to take care. You must select a topic that you have sufficient knowledge or research to write the essay easily. If you really want to make your essay interesting, good, and readable then you must avoid writing on topics that you are not familiar with and avoid writing away from the topic.

There are many things, which you need to avoid while you are writing an essay. The things, which you need to avoid, are as follow:

- Do not take topics which you are not familiar with or which you do not have knowledge of. Because if you do then this will surely give a bad impression of your essay simply because you will not be able to write anything meaningful or solid about the topic.
- Try to avoid spelling mistakes while you are writing the essay. Because sometimes what happens when you write your essay in a hurry then you are bound to make some spelling mistakes here and there.
- The third important mistake, which you need to avoid, is the grammatical error in your essay. Because this will play the main role in your essay. For instance, the grammar

mistake can change the sense of your content. So please try to avoid the grammatical error in your essay.

- Try to avoid writing very long-winded sentences and very lengthy paragraphs, as this will create boredom to your readers. Always write small paragraphs and meaningful content. This will help to make your essay more readable and interesting.
- Do not repeat the sentences because this will make a wrong séance in your readers mind. So always, try to write short, simple, and straight to the point sentences, which will help you to get your points across faster.
- The other most important mistake to avoid in essay writing is the criticism. Because this will create a wrong impression in the readers minds. So, try to avoid that.
- One last thing, which you need to avoid, is writing short lines. Do not make long sentences because this may change the sense of the whole line. So, try to avoid all these things from your essay to make your essay writing good.

If you can avoid the above mistakes in your essay, then your essay will be going and perfect. These are the tips to make your essay interesting and readable.

Quotes about Essays

Essays, entitled critical, are epistles addressed to the public, through which the mind of the recluse relieves itself of its impressions.

-Margaret Fuller

I love to run smart essays and commentary. But it doesn't replace the other kind of reporting.

-Tina Brown

I sort of was good at writing essays. I was never very good at mathematics, and I was never very good at algebra. I loved science, but I wasn't sure of it.

-Diane Cilento

I think the pattern of my essays is, A funny thing happened to me on my way through Finnegans Wake.

-Leslie Fiedler

I undertake the same project as Montaigne, but with an aim contrary to his own: for he wrote his Essays only for others, and I write my reveries only for myself.

-Jean-Jacques Rousseau

I won't say ours was a tough school, but we had our own coroner. We used to write essays like: What I'm going to be if I grow up.

-Lenny Bruce

I'm older than my sister so I started writing first. I started writing at school. I was always top of my class in composition, essays, English Lit and all of that.

-Joan Collins

In effect I am not a novelist, but rather a failed essayist who started to write novels because he didn't know how to write essays.

-Jose Saramago

Maybe I will write a memoir, perhaps I'll do some essays, or maybe I will write a mystery story.

-David Herbert Donald

Someone who can write aphorisms should not fritter away his time in essays.

-Karl Kraus

The essays are different because ultimately it's things I'm interested in, and I'm really just writing about myself and using those subjects as a prism.

-Chuck Klosterman

The essays are very solipsistic and self-absorbed, I'm totally conscious of that. To me, book writing is fun, and I basically just write about things that are entertaining to myself.

-Chuck Klosterman

The essays in *The Great Taos Bank Robbery* were my project to win a Master of Arts degree in English when I quit being a newspaper editor and went back to college.

-Tony Hillerman

There are some fine books and essays about that. Lewis Hyde has written about alcoholism and poets and the role that society gives its writers — encouraging them to die.

-Sharon Olds

To spend this particular year reading essays to Dennis Robertson as one's supervisor, and, simultaneously, enjoying membership of the group round Keynes was indeed an intellectual treat.

-James Meade

❖❖❖

2

Sample Essays

Importance of Yoga

Human beings are made up of three components—body, mind and soul corresponding these there are three needs—health, knowledge and inner peace. Health is physical need, knowledge is our psychological needs and inner peace is spiritual need when all three are present then there is harmony.

Yoga gives us relief from countless ailments at the physical level. The practice of the postures *(asans)* strengthen the body and create a feeling of well being. From the psychological view point, yoga sharpens the intellect and aid in concentration; it steadies the emotions and encourages a caring for others.

The practice of breathing techniques *(pranayam)* calms the mind. In the realm of the spiritual yoga brings awareness and the ability to be still. Through meditation inner peace is experienced. Thus, yoga is a practical philosophy involving every aspect of a person's being. It teaches the evolution of the individual by the development of self-discipline and self-awareness. Anyone irrespective of age, health circumstances of life and religion can practice yoga. Yoga helps to discipline our sense of power with the, power of our own.

If we peep into the benefits of yoga, they are numerous. It improve physical fitness, stress, controls general well being, mental clarity and greater self-understanding. People of all ages can do yoga and it can also be adapted for people with disabilities or special needs. The *asanas* enhance muscle strength, coordination, flexibility and can help to keep our body fit control cholesterol level, reduces weight, normalises blood pressure and improves cardiovascular performance.

Apart from these when people actively seek to reduce the stress in their lives by consoling the mind. The body often works to heal itself. In this sense yoga can be seen not only as a way to get into shape on several levels, but also as a tool for self-healing.

In today's world of information and inter planetary voyages most of the people find it difficult to devote time towards their health and fitness. This has led to drastic increase in health problems and health related stress—the number one killer in modern days. Unlike the early part of the century when infectious diseases were the leading killers, today's health problems are mostly related to life-style.

Cardiovascular, heart disease, stroke, chronic lung disease, diabetes, cirrhosis of liver, suicide and several forms of cancer are all related to unhealthy lifestyle and behaviour. At one point of time or the other, a doctor comes into the scene in every individual's life. Yoga is also self-diagnosis, healing prevention and maintenance. Although it is not replacement of one's doctor, yet it has been practiced safely and successfully by millions of people who never had doctors, for thousands of years. With the help of yoga the doctor and the individual can both monitor the progress and the doctor will definitely learn from individual how beneficial yoga really is.

In the context of self-diagnosis yoga postures and exercises can be easily done and that too with minimal possible effort. The magic of yoga is that as we begin the basic stretches we can immediately discover where our deficiencies are. If we are really up to, then we should not be discouraged by this.

We can do yoga, as perfectly as possible with a modest amount of care and patience, yoga triggers our body's natural adaptive and rejuvenating powers. Unless we use it we will lose it and if we start using it again we can get most of it back. Some people even claim that yoga gave them more vitality than they ever had in their lives. Even those who began later in life also benefited from its practice.

As for athletes or sports persons, yoga can be a powerful enhancement in regular training exercises. Adding yoga in a routine training programme helps develop strength, flexibility, range of motion, concentration, and cardiovascular health and reduces stress, tension and tightness. The most significant benefit of adding yoga to a training programme is its effect on performance. It allows an athlete to train harder and a higher level because of motion is greater and the fear of injury lessens.

Some people think it is divine others find it positively addictive and a powerfully effective substitute for negative habits. Whether borne of inspiration or by trial and error, yoga techniques substitute for the kinds of activities our early human ancestors must have done in the course of just living out in their arboreal lives. It is pretty to say that if we still hung around trees all our lives like other primates, then 70% to 90% of us would not end up suffering from chronic back, neck and head pain.

Obviously it takes time for our body to tuck itself in here and fill out there. Tissues have to grow. Others need to shrink. This is why it is important to drink lots of water and eats amount of wholesome food along with regular moderate exercise. In challenging those muscles to remodel themselves, we are literally clearing out lots of junks from our tissues.

The essence of yoga is to make the process of life as efficient and enjoyable as possible. In the beginning it is essential that we learn not only what the stretches are, but how to stretch, how to relax and how to breathe etc. Then we will be ready to work out safely, yoga does not bring away the qualities of genuinity, wholesomeness, compassion, but rather instills them within us. It teaches us that love heals the giver at least as much as it does the recipient. In addition therein dwells the sacred power of community, union, harmony, yoga and free and fair civilisation. It is our birth right to have access to this information. It is a sign of our wisdom if we use it, our enlightenment if we share it.

As we start practicing simple asanas we will immediately find out what needs attention the most while giving it the attention it calls for. The effects are immediate and the results keep becoming more apparent. The longer and more often we engage in the pure self-indulgent healing art of yoga. The more it will have a healing effect on us. Yoga is no less magical than the power of life itself. It unlocks life's wonder and unleashes hidden energies.

Through this art everyone can experience the Divine and enjoy the ecstasy of freedom from pain and ignorance apart from other gracious rewards like longevity and happiness. It has taken time for us to wind ourselves up in a knot. Naturally it takes time to unravel. If we are still breathing, it is never too soon or late to start yoga.

Democracy and Discipline

Democracy without discipline is a body without soul. If there is no discipline in the country, democracy will degenerate into a monocracy i.e., a Government by a unruly crowd. In fact, in Greek 'Demos' means crowd. The word 'curacy' is from the Greek word 'Krait' or 'Cratos' which means power. A lack of discipline in democracy justifies Plato's criticism that democracy is the divine right of the ignorant people to rule ignorantly.

It is true that democracy is based on the free will of the people who are supreme and sovereign. But this does not mean that democracy grants absolute liberty to the people to do anything. Under this mistaken belief, some people misuse their rights and liberties. Not only that, some people also think wrongly that in a democracy they have only rights but no duties. These people do not know that rights and duties go hand-in-hand.

No doubt, under a democratic form of government, people enjoy the freedom to elect their representatives in accordance with their wishes at the time of election. Even after the election, they can always make their views on various issues known to the Government through the press, radio or T.V. But they must air their grievances through constitutional and non-violent means. If people take the law in their own hands and become violent, they will neither deserve democracy nor can they make a success of it.

Everything is fair in love and war but it is not so in a

democracy. Democracy calls for a high degree of discipline, respect for the views of others and unflinching faith in equality, fairly and justice. Mahatma Gandhi had stressed the need for spiritualizing our politics by inculcating moral discipline among the people. According to him, democracy does not mean simply the grant of rights and their enjoyment. If the people want to enjoy their rights they must be prepared to perform their duties as well.

We find that in the world only those countries whose people are disciplined have made progress and achieved greatness. Although the economies of Japan and West Germany were completely shattered during the Second World War, they were able to rebuild their countries due to the dedicated work of their disciplined citizens. They have achieved great success in science, technology and industry.

But for the sense of discipline in their people, they would not have been able to achieve such success. Both Japan and Germany are democratic countries. They have, by their example, shown to the world that if democracy and discipline go hand in hand, countries can make great progress.

On the other hand, if a country lacks discipline, it is bound to be doomed and eventually to be replaced by a dictatorship. The people will then lose their freedom of thought and action. They will have to carry out the orders of the dictator. They will have no say whatsoever in the administration of the country.

Only in those democratic countries which are inhabited by disciplined people, can the citizens enjoy the fruits of democracy. For example, in Switzerland, people are so disciplined and hard-working that they have made their country synonymous with democracy. They have become prosperous by dint of their disciplined and industrious temperament.

In India, we have rightly adopted a democratic form of Government. It is now up to us, the people of India, to imbibe the spirit of discipline and to make democracy a grand success. For this, we should make a beginning by teaching discipline to our children at home itself and laying stress on it in the schools of the country, because the children of today are the future citizens of our country. If they are taught discipline today, then tomorrow they can be disciplined citizens and can make our country strong, united and powerful.

Nowadays we are hearing about a lot of indiscipline and lawlessness in many parts of our country by certain vested interests that are guided and inspired by certain inimical foreign powers. These misguided and indiscipline people do not know what great harm they are causing to the unity of our country by their secessionist acts. They should remember that if India remains united and strong they will also live a prosperous life. On the other hand, if India as a whole is weakened and divided they will also perish with it. So the success or failure of India is in reality the success or failure of her people.

Therefore, it is the foremost duty of all citizens of India to remain united and disciplined, to defeat the designs of foreign powers to destroy the unity of India and the democratic set-up of our country. By discipline and unity alone can democracy prosper in our country, and we remain free.

Urbanization in India

Urbanization means concentration of population leading to high density of population in big cities. As per the 2011 census, more than 377 million people live in urban areas. Urbanization is posing serious problems even in the advanced countries of the world. These problems are congestion, industrialization, environmental pollution, insanitation, lack of civic amenities, bottlenecks in free flow of traffic, etc.

The main reason for the growth of population in big cities is the migration of people from the villages to the cities in search of employment. Cities provide greater opportunities of employment, better living conditions and higher standard of living to the villagers. Cities also provide entertainment through the cinema, theatre, television, hotels, etc. Thus once a villager comes to the city, he never thinks of going back to his village.

Due to concentration of population, the big cities become the dens of crime and corruption. Take, for instance, U.S.A. In its big cities, a number of organised criminal gangs have come into existence.

Urbanization leads to shortage of houses in big cities. This shortage, in turn, pushes up the prices of land to astronomical heights. The pressure of population in big cities also causes haphazard growth, setting up of unauthorised colonies by unscrupulous elements, mushroom growth of juggins and creation of slums.

Urbanization creates bottlenecks in the free flow of traffic. There is an unending stream of buses, trucks, tempos, scooters, motor cycles, cycles and pedestrians especially during the peak hours. Not only in metros but also in other cities, traffic jams have become a part of city life.

The Municipal authorities are not able to cope with the situation. Urbanization causes breakdown of civil services. The Municipal authorities are not in a position to provide clean drinking water to the entire population throughout the day. Supply of electricity to the people gets disrupted every now and then. The drains are not cleaned regularly.

Urbanization leads to growth in demand but shortage of supply of various commodities. Traders exploit the situation of shortage and indulge in adulteration. No one can get pure milk or pure food in big cities. This adversely affects the health of the city dwellers. The people in big cities lead a very fast and busy life. They suffer from hypertension, anxiety and fear. They hardly have any peace of mind.

Of course, urbanization has certain merits also. First, the big cities have a large number of schools and colleges for imparting education. By acquiring education, people in cities are able to gain knowledge and get gainful employment. Secondly, all big cities have well-equipped hospitals where people suffering from various diseases can go for diagnosis and treatment. Thirdly, the big cities provide a wide range of means of entertainment. Fourthly, the scientific and technological progress of a country depends on its big cities because these cities possess facilities for advanced research and development.

In short, while urbanization has some merits, it has also given rise to a number of problems. In fact, the government should give concessional loans for establishing labour intensive industries so that more people can get employment in rural areas itself. Better educational facilities should be provided so that people living in rural areas do not move to cities in order to take education. This will go a long way to stop the urbanization. If rural people are provided better living conditions like supply of fresh water, road connecting villages with cities, electricity, etc. then there is no reason why urbanization cannot be stopped. The Government is trying its best to develop satellite towns around metropolitan cities to avoid congestion and pollution in the big cities.

India might be adding to its number of billionaires but slum population in urban cities is increasing rapidly with nearly one-third of the urban population being poor. An independent study by NGO Urban Health Resource Centre (UHRC) has found that nearly 30% or 90 million people living in urban areas are poor and according to UNHABITAT, the number is likely to touch 200 million in 2020.

By 2030, an estimated 5 billion of the world's 8.1 billion people will live in cities. About 2 billion of them will live in slums, primarily in Africa and Asia, lacking access to clean drinking water and working toilets, surrounded by desperation and crime. Already there slums are huge according to Mike Davis, author of *Planet of Slums*, nearly 80% of Nigeria's urban population or some 41.6 million people, and live in slums. The comparable numbers in India are 56% and 158.4 million. Many of these slum dwellers are also squatters, lacking leases or legal title to their homes.

Co–education

In ancient times, co-education was prevalent in Sparta, a city-state of Greece. Both boys and girls were given academic education and physical training together. There was no discrimination between the boys and the girls. They played and studied together.

Plato, the Greek philosopher, was also in favour of co-education. He believed that co-education helped in the development of personality of men and women and created a feeling of comradeship between them. He felt that coeducation was the only method to make both men and women useful members of society. In ancient India also boys and girls were brought up and taught together. They were not segregated from each other.

Nowadays, the system of co-education is in vogue in U.S.A., Europe and other advanced countries of the world. In India also, a number of co-educational schools and colleges have been established.

There are a number of advantages in the co-educational system of education. Firstly, if boys and girls are taught together in the same school under the same roof, there will be no need to open separate schools for girls. A poor country like India cannot afford the luxury of opening separate schools for boys and girls. Co-education is thus economical.

Secondly, there is a shortage of trained teachers in India. If the same staff teaches boys and girls together, we can manage with the existing staff of teachers.

Thirdly, if boys and girls study in separate schools, they will grow up in watertight compartments. The result will be that girls will feel shy in the presence of boys. Boys will have curiosity about girls. Co-education helps the boys and girls to inter-mingle and understand each other well. It leads to harmonious relationship between boys and girls.

Fourthly, co-education generates healthy competition between boys and girls. Both boys and girls work hard to remain ahead of each other in studies and sports.

Fifthly, co-education creates a feeling of comradeship between boys and girls. As the boys are free to meet and talk to the girls, they do not indulge in eve-teasing. Girls too do not feel shy in the presence of boys. The system co-education is thus very conducive to the balanced development of the personality of boys and girls.

However, there are some conservative people who are opposed to system of co-education. They point out that this system is against our tradition and culture. They apprehend that if boys and girls study together, the possibility of their developing immoral relationship cannot be ruled out. They also felt that the system of co-education may spoil the character of boys and girls.

But these arguments are not very convincing and do not hold well in modern times. If our experience is any guide, boys dress properly and behave well in the company of girls. They use dignified language. By nature, boys are curious about girls. If they study with girls, their curiosity will be satisfied. They will not regard girls as strange creatures. Likewise, if girls are taught with boys, they will not feel shy. They will understand boys better.

Thus, we can say that the advantages of the system of co-education outweigh the disadvantages. Since the boys and the girls have to, later on, live together as husband and wife, there is no point in segregating them in schools or colleges. We should move with the times and open more and more coeducational institutions in India. The hackneyed morality of the medieval ages should not be allowed to stand in the way of the progress of our youth who are the future citizens of India.

Benefits of Positive Thinking

Positive thinking is the belief that good things will happen and that one's efforts will be crowned with success. It is something diametrically opposed to negative thinking which is being fearful, apprehensive and unsure of success in efforts. Positive thinking is based on optimism, hope and belief that hard work is never wasted. The effects of positive thinking are magical. Psychologists believe that nothing gears up people to make whole-hearted efforts to perform some task as positive thinking.

The feeling tones up every muscle of the body and activates every nerve of the mind for a perfect coordination between the body and the mind to do the job when hope enlivens a human being; his/her efforts become focused and earnest. The vision of achievement and the glory or appreciation associated with it propels a person to work in such a way that no stone is left unturned to achieve the desired goal.

Positive thinking helps a person find a way in a difficult task or a tough situation. He starts feeling that something can be done to overcome the difficulties that are looming large at that moment. It is said that a serious person finds a way, while an idler finds an excuse. The difference between these two is that of attitude-of being hopeful or being without hope. A person who keeps hopes alive gives himself a chance to succeed, however difficult the task. He puts in earnest endeavours. He may get favour of luck, and help may come from unexpected quarters. On the other hand, a person who loses hope can never make a whole-hearted effort. His battle is half lost even before the start.

It is said that life is not a bed of roses. Each person has to face difficult situation in his life. If one becomes fearful and apprehensive about the results, feelings of frustration, depression and disappointment will enter his mind and hinder his normal faculties of working. He may even end up poorer than he actually is. In the present age of tough competition nothing is given by the world on a platter.

Those who do not put in the required amount of efforts are left behind to suffer and repent. 'Hope sustains life' is an old, time-tested adage. It accentuates the importance of positive thinking. If you do not think positively you may lose the initiative to do well to achieve your objectives. Positive thinking builds will power. People have reached dizzy heights by sheer will power supported by hard work. When there is will there is a way is not an idle statement. It contains a lot of substance.

History is full of examples that show that people have achieved amazing results by perseverance and positive attitude. King Bruce of Scotland could not free his land despite many efforts. He had to run away and hide in a cave. He saw a spider who was trying to reach the roof. It made nine attempts but each time it fell just before making it. It tried again and succeeded to reach the roof. King Bruce learnt a great lesson of keeping the hope alive. He made a concerted attempt and was able to free his land. Columbus had no money or fleet of ships to make a voyage across the globe. But he was sure that one day he will be able to realize his dream.

He approached many people for help. Ultimately, the king of Italy helped him. He made his historic voyage and discovered America. Louis Pasteur saw people dying of dog bite-with rabies. He was sure that he would prepare a vaccine to fight this malady. He worked hard and prepared anti-rabies vaccine. Humanity owes him a lot to save the lives of millions who have been treated of rabies all over the world. When India won the Cricket World Cup in 1983, the West Indies team was the strongest in the world. India defeated it even after scoring only 183 runs batting first. India's captain Kapil Dev told his teammates that anything is possible in cricket. If we fight hard, keep self-belief, we may win the match. And it actually happened. India became the champions.

The feat was repeated by the young Indian side under M.S. Dhoni's captaincy to win the Twenty-20 World Cup. Abraham

Lincoln fought many elections in a row. He could not win even a single election. But hope sprang eternal in him. He contested the presidential election and won. He became the President of America. Such examples are endless. All of them go on to show the major role positive thinking plays in our success. It is pertinent to mention here that mere positive thinking without putting in the required amount of effort will not lead to success.

We need to make a proper assessment of the task in hand, prepare a plan of action finding, the right method to perform it, and then make an integrated endeavour. Applying wrong methods even with positive thinking will result into the failure. Depending entirely on hope or unexpected help or a stroke of luck is foolishness not positive thinking.

Hope is secondary to efforts. Positive thinking therefore essentially means to be hopeful of a good result after making the required effort. It is an attitude to go for the performance of a task with a hope that it can be done. It also means to be confident of success in a difficult situation hoping that even such a situation can be controlled if we do what it takes. Efforts are the base on which hope is built; without the required amount of efforts, endeavour or hard work-whatever you call it, no one can be sure of success.

An important question that arises in this regard is: Is positive thinking an inherent characteristic of a person or can it be developed in one's psyche? The opinions differ in answering this vital question.

Some people believe that it can be inherited from parents, and cannot be developed. Others believe that like other qualities it can be developed with proper practice and guidance. Still some others hold the opinion that it is hereditary to some extent but can be acquired to some degree. There is also a section of people who believe that all depends on circumstances or luck. Some people are born lucky. They get success with minimum effort; others don't get it even after greatest of endeavour. There are, thus, various theories and opinions based on one's experience and knowledge.

We need to adopt a scientific approach to find an answer to the above question. No one can get success every time even after making efforts, nor can one fail constantly. Moreover, success has different meanings for different people. For some students getting 60 per cent marks is success, for others it may not be sufficient. In a competitive examination success means getting selected, whatever the percentage of marks.

As for inheritance theory, since positive attitude is not a physical feature but a mental faculty it cannot be purely hereditary. It can be developed. Moreover, parents play a major role in a child developing this quality. A child who watches his parents work hard, showing hope of success through their words, behaviour and body language is likely to develop a similar attitude.

The children of short tempered, over cautious and nervous parents may assume these characteristics when they grow up. Psychologists therefore prescribe a code of conduct for parents' behaviours in front of their offspring. They must exude confidence, self-belief and hope, especially in difficult situation, so that the children emulate these qualities. They must be taught the importance of being positive before, during and after the performance of a task. There is no better education for a child than watching his/her parents come out of a tough situation by means of earnest endeavours. Such success not only gives more joy, increases self-confidence and acts as an object lesson for children and younger members in the family.

The role of teachers in building the confidence of students and telling them about the importance of positive thinking is also vital; the teachers encourage hard work by appreciating and rewarding those who make it. They rebuke and warn those who are not serious in their studies. They tell students about the various ways in which they can improve their scoreline. Prizes, certificates, awards, etc. are aimed at appreciating hard work that precedes good performance.

In the modern age of science there are many other ways like yoga, meditation, exercises, reading of inspiring books which can relieve us of tension, worry and make us relaxed and hopeful.

Science–A Blessing or Curse

This is the age of science and technology. Science has changed the face of the earth with its too many wonderful inventions and discoveries. If one of our ancestors were to return to the earth, he or she would not be able to recognize it—so tremendous, complete and fundamental has been the change.

Science has benefited mankind in an unprecedented manner by its wonderful progress and development. And still the development, research, inventions and discoveries are going on a very fast track. These are of fundamental nature and of far reaching consequences, so much so that the world would get further transformed unrecognizably.

Science touches all of us and our life at every step, as a big boon and blessing. It has helped us to conquer space and time. The world has now become a global village, thanks to very fast and reliable means of travel and communication. Science has also helped man to conquer the moon and to explore the outer space. Many a fatal disease is now checked and eradicated. For example, small pox is now a disease of the history only. The great and significant researches in the fields, of agriculture, irrigation, water-management, etc., have helped in developing new variety of seeds, fertilizers, pesticides, and effective methods of water conservation. These benefits and facilities were not available to our forefathers.

The use of computers and super computers has further revolutionised our life and work with the dawn of scientific era, the barriers of the nations are crumbling fast and the international living and interaction are very much in sight. Nations and countries have come closer and isolation has been eliminated. A new composite culture marked with greater tolerance and understanding, and secularism is now assured. In a sense, science has unified the world and reduced differences in outlook and thinking. By removing many superstitions and blind beliefs, modern science has inculcated scientific temper and spirit in man to great extent.

Because of science and technology there has been tremendous progress in the fields of industry, commerce and human resources development as well. Consequently, there is a new world economic order in sight and the gap between the developed and developing countries are being reduced. The new economic order ensures a great industrial and corporate cooperation, globalization, expansion and liberalization among the nations. The quality of life and standard of living, in various underdeveloped and developing counties, have improved and the countries are likely to be upgraded further. The contribution of science in the betterment of human life has been great and significant and further expectations from it are no less significant or great. The boons and blessings of science assure us further strengthening of human equality, fraternity and liberty.

Man feels more safe, secure, comfortable and important. Today than ever before, because of scientific development and advancement. The day is not far off when we shall have colonies on the moon and the planets. Science has achieved much, and promises to achieve still more and more in the years to come. Science has tamed forces of nature, conquered space and time, eradicated may fatal diseases, given us food, clothing etc., and enough to spare. Now there are no more famines, epidemics and pestilences. Science has even pushed further the threats of death and increased the average longevity of man.

But science has been a mixed blessing. It has been a boon and blessing in certain fields; it has also proved a curse and bane in many others. It has given us many dangerous and destructive weapons like atom and hydrogen bombs and missiles. During the Second World War itself 300,000 people died in Hiroshima and Nagasaki when the USA dropped atom bombs there in 1945. The biological and chemical weapons are still more destructive. The bombs and other means of mass destruction now produced are far more lethal and powerful than used in 1945. The biological and chemical weapons are still more dangerous and destructive. They have the added advantage, as the source of attack can remain hidden and unidentified to a great extent. These weapons can be used to cause global havoc and destruction without any open declaration of war. Then there are well-organized terrorist groups spread all over the world. They use these weapons in their desperation and use unprecedented deaths and ruination.

Shakespeare has said that there is nothing either good or bad, but thinking makes it so. There have been many scientific researches and discoveries which have unfortunately been hijacked to harmful destructive paths. It is reported that about half a million scientists are now employed on weapon research throughout the world. The huge amount of money spent on these dangerous researches fan exceeds the amount of money being spent on developing technologies for new energy resources, improving human health, raising agricultural productivity, controlling pollution, etc.

At the end of the last world war, many of the scientists were taken away by the victorious countries for developing their own biological and chemical war weapons. It is alleged that the outbreak of plague in India in 1994 was genetically engineered.

Obviously, science is being used so much for destructive purposes and so little for meeting real needs of humanity. This turns science into a bane. It is man who is ultimately responsible for turning science into a curse instead a blessing. By itself science can be said to be a blessing, boon or bonanza; the bane and cures are brought about by our wrong orientation and priorities.

The misuse of science has ushered in our life many undesirable elements. There has been erosion in man's faith in Sod and religion. Morality and ethics have been marginalized and materialism has increased unprecedented. Rapid, unplanned and indiscriminate industrialization has resulted in pollution on a vast scale. No doubt, science and technology has taken giant strides in recent times, but it has dehumanized human life in the same proportion.

Human values have been pushed in the background and man has become more selfish, cruel, sensual, violent and destructive. There is no more simple living and high thinking.

But let us hope that ultimately sanity prevails and science is used more and more for the benefit of mankind. It depends solely upon man himself how he uses science and its discoveries and researches. Science as knowledge and power is neither savior nor destroyer.

Status of Women in India

There has been a marked change for the better in our existing, over-all approach towards the women. Gone are the days when their place was considered to be behind the four walls of the house and their only job was confined to looking after the household affairs. But now they can be seen working shoulder to shoulder with men in every sphere of life.

We had a highly successful and efficient woman Prime Minister, late Mrs. Indira Gandhi, in addition to having many women governors and Chief Ministers. And even in our own time, there is no dearth of women judges, lawyers, doctors, administrators, police officers and engineers.

This is, undoubtedly, a good sign and an indication of their emancipation. This has, however, increased the workload of working women manifold. They attend to their official juries and after eight hours of testing and nerve-breaking office duty, return home to a different kind of job.

It is a common sight to see them hurrying back from their offices in the evening only to enter the kitchen at home and cook for the family and attend to other domestic chores. It is the same picture in rural areas. After toiling on the farms, they go back home to do all the household chores.

The men, whether in the urban or in the rural areas, seldom help in the household tasks. This situation exists because men regard themselves as superior in mental and physical power to women. Similarly, women too have been made to accept their subordinate position. However, it is rather surprising that this type of wrong thinking has not changed with the changing times.

This attitude of superiority on the part of men has caused many problems for working women. In offices, though they are selected to important positions, they often have to prove themselves doubly competent in order to get a promotion. Again their absence from duty or late arrival is frowned upon, whereas the same lapse in a male colleague is, generally, ignored and over-looked.

Even in day-to-day routine-life, women have to face a host of problems because the basic attitude towards them still remains unchanged. Customs which downgrade the position of women have yet to be overcome. The dowry system is one such custom. If the girl's parents are unable to arrange for it, the girl is harassed or sent back to her parental home or sometimes even burnt to death.

Another area where women have yet to get equality is in property matters. The law has been changed to provide equal property rights to the son and daughter in a family. But this is only on paper, and the daughter gracefully relinquishes her share in the property. If she insists on getting it, she is forced to go to court, for it is seldom given as a matter of right.

The very birth of a female member in a family is still an occasion to mourn, whereas the birth of a son is celebrated with great pomp and show. The present 'uplifted' status of women has put them between the devil and the deep sea.

Or, one hand, they seem to have been liberated to the extent that they are working outside, side by side with men, but, on the other hand, they have to face a number of problems because of this very fact. What are the solutions to these problems?

The law has, however, been amended in favour of women in many cases. Thus eave-teasing in public places, harassment in office, the dowry problem, property rights etc. can be dealt with in the court, yet the basic problem would remain unsolved. This is related to the attitude of the people, and unless this is changed, women, on the whole, would remain deprived of their rights as well as justice.

Educational institutions can help by teaching equality of the sexes through the lessons. Further, the family too should not be biased and give the same kind of upbringing to the sons and daughter. Boys should be made to help as much as the girls in domestic chores.

The mass media should also project the picture of the women as an equal with man, having the same desired ambitions and intelligence. True liberation of women possible only when our over-all attitude is changed.

Pollution

It is an established fact that our metro cities are not good enough to live in. They offer neither pure, safe drinking water, nor a healthy, fresh air to breathe. The noise of ever-increasing number of vehicles does not allow us to sleep even at night.

All our important cities have been found to be the worst polluted cities in the world. It is, therefore, not surprising that major health problems have become recurring occurrences. In order to overcome the problem, it is important to identify the sources of pollution.

The major source of pollution in the cities is the heavy traffic on the roads. Buses, cars, motor-cycles and other such vehicles emit carbon mono-oxide, which badly affects our lungs.

In fact, sometimes, it becomes difficult even to breathe because one can feel the heavy air that one is inhaling. Another source of pollution is the smoke from the factories, running in residential areas. They emit highly toxic fumes into the atmosphere making life miserable for those who live around.

Another reason of too much pollution is the absence of plants and trees. Cutting down of trees indiscriminately everywhere for the sake of buildings has created the problem of survival itself. We forget that trees breathe in carbon-dioxide and release oxygen into the atmosphere so that the atmosphere is, automatically, purified.

However, the blind race for industrialization and development everywhere has resulted in very few patches of greenery in our cities. It has resulted in our suffering the ill-effects of atmospheric pollution.

Water is another essential necessity which, again, we get in a highly polluted form. It is easy to isolate the sources of pollution here also. One reason is our age-old superstitious belief in ancient customs which leads us to make the water filthy. For example, hair after a 'Mundan' ceremony is collected and thrown into the river Ganges or the Yamuna.

Ashes and left-over bones, after the cremation of the dead body of a friend or relative, are also thrown into these and other big rivers. It never comes to our mind that the cities, through which these rivers are flowing, receive their water supply from them. Yet people can be seen washing their dirty clothes with impunity on the banks of these rivers which further contaminates the water.

As if all this is not enough, effluents from industries are also released into the rivers and these further aggravate the problem. Yet again, the pipes through which the water is supplied to us are often old and rusted. There is apparently no way of cleaning them with the result that worms, cysts, dust, and other impurities are a normal part of the 'fresh' water, supplied to us in the cities.

The aftermath of all this pollution of air and water is really deadly for all those living in cities. Air pollution leaves no pure air to breathe in and these results in a host of diseases like suffocation, breathlessness, asthma and migraine.

The body remains deprived of its required supply of oxygen and thus we feel too weak to work efficiently. This is why our cities are filled with pale, anemic-looking adults and children, for the blood deprived of the life-giving oxygen, absorbs the toxic gases present in the atmosphere.

Water pollution is also highly harmful. In addition to the toxic effects of the industrial poisons, which the water contains, cysts and worms have become a chronic problem with many a city dweller. Even heavy chlorination shows no beneficial effects and the level of pollution remains above the acceptable norms.

No wonder, epidemics like cholera, typhoid, hepatitis and other such water-borne diseases regularly attack the masses. Further, the dust, which can easily be seen, if the water is collected in a vessel and left standing for sometime, results in the bladder and kidney problems.

The most urgent need of the hour, therefore, is to have an effective check on the pollution problem, if we are to escape being a nation of sick and unhealthy citizens. This is possible only when individuals and the government are serious enough about remedying the situation and make quick, joint efforts.

A number of steps are to be initiated to get rid of the air-pollution in cities. All of us should maintain our vehicles well so that only the minimum amount of fumes is emitted. The government can take a strong view of it and penalize the offenders heavily. If there are frequent checks, they are sure to yield positive results.

Again, there should be continuous check on the industries, spewing smoke and toxic fumes without any consideration for others into the atmosphere. The chimneys should be at a height from where the smoke does not come down to the earth. Wherever possible, trees and plants should be planted. This will convert the carbon-di-oxide in the atmosphere in to life-giving oxygen.

Likewise, stern and deterring steps must be taken to check water pollution. Dumping of rubbish at any point in any river has to be prohibited. To respect the religious sentiments of the people, certain areas could be cordoned-off for the ceremonial disposal of ashes etc. A regular cleaning operation of the river should be undertaken.

The results are sure to be highly rewarding, if mass involvement is encouraged. Sometime back there was a major Ganges-Cleaning Operation, and it yielded tonnes of rubbish. However, unless this is done on a regular basis, the problem is not going to be eliminated forever.

Again, the industries throwing their waste into the river-waters should be ordered to incinerate it at the source. Further the municipal authority's in-charge of the water supply should clean up their tanks regularly and filter and treat the water properly to free it from dust, cysts and other dangerous matter in it. Epidemics of water-borne diseases would, then, be prevented from increasing at the source.

Importance of Education

According to Bacon "Reading makes a full man; writing an exact man and conference a ready man." And if someone asks what reading, writing and conference make together, anyone would say that all of them stand for Education. In other words, we can say that education makes anyone complete, accurate and worldly wise. It means that no one is complete without education.

Thus, we can confidently say that education is necessary an all-round development of the personality of a human-being. He cannot hope for success, name, fame and prosperity in life without it.

Even a nation would be devoid of any progress, if its citizens fail to have the benefits of education. H.L. Wayland has correctly said, "Universal suffrage, without universal education, would be a curse." For the success of any democracy, education is a must. Imagine a country with illiterate ministers voted to power by illiterate people!

Unfortunately, there are many people who downgrade the value of education and say that it has never benefited anyone. But this is not correct. Knowledge is too far advanced today for a man to gain without its specialized branch. Trade, industry, agriculture, medicine, the I.T. and all other areas have become so complex that no one can take up any job without being educated.

An educated man will never find himself stranded in the midst of any difficulty. His brain, developed by serious-thinking during his academic years, will unfailingly arrive at some solution to the problem that besets him. This is what education prepares us for. And most of all, education gives us not only the mental but also physical strength necessary to face any challenges of life with dignity.

An illiterate person simply gropes in the dark, leaving result to chance or fate. He is ultimately dependent on others. Farmers in India, in olden times, who could not read or write, were cheated out of their land and willingly suffered exploitation and injustice only because they had no education.

They were deprived of their rights by unscrupulous landlords, moneylenders and middlemen, who made them, put their thumb impressions on false documents of possession. Women in India had been suppressed, dominated and ill-treated only because they had no education.

But now with their having been educated to a certain extent, the old situation has started changing quite fast. Now they have come out in the open to fight for their rights. They are not dependent on others, nor do they silently submit to whatever cruelty is meted out to them.

Education liberates a man's mind from wrong thinking, ignorance, superstitions and prejudices. It frees him from evil influences and vices. It equips him with knowledge and skill, enabling him to make a good living, culminating in his being an ideal citizen.

With the spread of education, gone are the days of bonded labour, economic slavery, pangs on account of being an untouchable and being misled by black magic. Thus it can be boldly claimed that education has awakened the masses all over the world.

Dowry System

The Concise Oxford dictionary gives the following meaning of the word 'dowry': "Portion woman brings to her husband, talent, and natural gift." We stick to only the first meaning of the word and we forget altogether the second meaning.

Even the meaning of dowry as we understand it today is not so relevant or as irrelevant as we have made it through our vicious practices. Most probably the practice of giving of dowry by the girl's parent to the bridegroom originated in a noble spirit. Its purpose was to enable the newly wedded couple to start their household comfortably and with least inconvenience. But it all depended upon the capacity and will of girl's parents. There was no compulsion or coercion involved in it.

Unfortunately, in modern times, the dowry system has assumed alarming proportions. Dowry is given and taken freely. The boys are auctioned, as if, in the open market. They go to the highest bidders. The girls are treated as commodities or as cows and goats. No attention is paid to their natural gifts, their education and accomplishments. The poor fathers of the girls have to get themselves ground in the mills of sweat, toil and sacrifice all their lives. Thus the birth of a daughter becomes the bane and stigma to the unlucky father.

Even after having given a handsome dowry after begging, borrowing and stealing, the woes of poor parents do not end there. The girls are asked by their greedy in-laws to bring more and more gifts. In fact, there are endless demands. Many girls at last get bored and bold enough to raise a tremulous voice against cruel and unjust demands. The result is torture by the in-laws and in some cases even death by burning.

We claim to live in a civilised society. Often we flaunt our moralistic and idealistic pretensions. Should we not be ashamed of ourselves for practicing or letting practiced such cruel practices as the dowry system? If we have any qualms of conscience that prick us, should not we raise a full-throated voice against such barbaric practices?

As a first step, all of us should pledge never to give or take dowry in any form. Better to remain unmarried than to participate in such an obnoxious system. Secondly, we should socially boycott the defaulters. Thirdly, mustering up courage, we should report the matter to the police in case of default of the Anti-Dowry Act passed by the Parliament and the state legislatures. Fourthly, the women organizations should, in particular, activate themselves further and, if need be, sit in dharma in front of the houses of dowry seekers. In fact, this evil has taken such deep and firm roots in our society that only a determined bid and effort can uproot it.

My Aim in Life

Everybody has some aims in life. It is very important. A life without an aim is like a boat without a rudder. But choosing a career in such a cut throat age of competition is really a difficult task.

Different people have different aims in their life according to their tastes and temperament. Some people want to become technocrats like doctors, engineers, scientists while many want to become bureaucrats like IAS, IPS and IFS.

Some dream to become educationists, while for others politics holds great attraction. A few are lured to pursue their career in anti-social activities. There are people who have a craze to become poets, writers and novelists. To say, different people, different choices.

I am not a highly ambitious man. I am modest by nature. I do not want to be a multi-millionaire. The profession of teaching has been very attractive to me. This has been my childhood dream. The sole aim of my life is to serve the society to become a good citizen. To me teaching appears to be the best way to serve the society.

I belong to the lower middle class of society. Naturally, I have to face several difficulties in my life. The difficulties encountered during the journey of my life made me realise that lack of education is the biggest problem to which I will devote my life to spread literacy to every nook and corner of society so as to remove the darkness of illiteracy. It is a shame that one-fourth of our population still do not know how to read and write even after over six decades of independence. In terms of women education, the picture is all the more gloomy. Unless we are educated we cannot make all around progress.

I would be particularly sensitive to the needs of the weaker sections of society. I would work hard to bring change in their lives. When this section of society is educated, we will have a totally different society. There will be no superstitions when they will be educated. I will always be available to attend their queries whatever arise. I will arrange extra classes for those who find it difficult to keep pace with the regular class.

I am fully aware that I'll have to face lots of hardships. A teacher's life is hard. He does not command the respect he deserves. This profession is looked down upon as of a lowly status. A teacher's life is full of drudgery. I will not be concerned for the earnings. I will try my best to make the students good citizens. I will help them in broadening their outlook. I'll groom their personality and shape their characters. I'll try to inculcate in them good moral values. So that India have good citizens to take it on the path of progress and prosperity in which everyone has a dignified life full of equality of opportunities. According to great educationist and our former president Dr. S. Radhakrishnan, "Teachers are the custodians of the highest values."

Agriculture in India – Prospects and Challenges

Essay on Agriculture in India—Prospects and Challenges. The burgeoning billion plus population of India needs the best of modern agriculture techniques to keep track of the produce in the same ratio.

Agriculture is the prime prime pivot of the Indian economy contributing 30 per cent of the Gross Domestic Product. We have been lucky to have had a normal monsoon cycle over the last decade which has largely contributed to the food-grain production crossing the 200 million tonnes target. However, the rapid increase in the population level, expected to touch the 130 crore mark in the next two decades, needs an equally increased production of food grains and it is being planned to reach 275 million tones in period. The scenario is very bleak and getting more bleak every year. We have a population which is nearly 17 per cent of the total human population of the world and the arable land mass is just 2.2 per of the arable land. The per capita arable land area was 0.48 ha in 1950 which has now gone down to 0.14 ha in 2002. We have to manage our production of grain and other agricultural produce within this limitation. Instead of a horizontal growth we have to plan a graph on the basis of innovations like shorter durations and diversifications.

The earlier experiments of optimum use of fertilizers and

pesticides, which had ushered in the green revolution, has now started taking its toll. The soil has absorbed the maximum it could and the percentage of crops vis-à-vis chemicals used has started a steep decline. It has also resulted in toxic chemicals, via pesticides, polluting the crops, air and ground water. These are now finding its way into the human constitution creating further problems. Bio-degradation has been analysed as the result of contamination due to heavy metals like mercury, lead and fertilizers.

The unplanned discharge of sewage from industries is also finding its way to the soil and groundwater. The latest researches in D.A.N technology has made it possible to select genes and introduce the produce the productive ones into hybrid seeds with better productivity and nutritional value. Tissue culture is now one of the most important researches in bio-technology and has helped in introducing genetically modified plants with immense commercial value. The agriculture scenario is faced today with the discussed problems of low productivity, harmful and inferior crop quality and environmental pollution.

This is the reason that the best efforts of our agriculture scientists have failed to increase productivity, in certain crops, over the last few decades. But the latest techniques employed like photosynthetic activity, calculation of salt and moisture tolerance, overcoming fertiliser fatigue and resistance to pests and diseases are definitely going to be a boon. They have also succeeded in the early detection of crop infection through secondary metabolism, which will help the farmers in taking timely steps to their crops. The method is changing now and instead of solely depending on fertilizers, the use of organic and green manures are being propagated for maintenance of soil-health and an eco-friendly environment. Chemical pesticides are now being increasingly reduced and bio-friendly ones likes neem, saal and mahua, insects friendly to the crops but deadly for the pests, are being recommended. IPM or integral Pest Management is now the buzzword.

Training is also being imparted in timely removal of weeds and crop residues through surface ploughing. Mixed cropping and diversified agriculture is the need of the time. This is a planned branching of the facilities available and inter-related activities such as fish farming, forestry, piggery, poultry farming, bee keeping, sericulture etc. The small farmers are being imparted technical and financial knowledge in planning one or more such ventures in addition to cropping for better returns. The majors in farming have also entered diversifications

Farming of vegetables and oil-seeds and pulses are in the category of rotatory cropping, helping in the utilization of farms in a planned manner. However, the monopoly of the middle men and whole sellers in the market have been the reason why the actual farmers, specially the smaller ones, do not get their requisite return. These are being sold at price 400 per cent more than what the farmer actually gets in the market. The consumer and the farmer and both losers in the bargain whereas the middlemen heavily line their pockets.

Another major disadvantage we face is a proper system of storage for food grains purchased by the government agencies like Food Corporation of India. Our storage agencies are brimming over with stocks of nearly 75 million tones, of which half are rotting away, not even being fit for use as cattle fodder.

This inglorious wastage of precious food grain, even as humans die starvation death in the interior, is a sad reflection of our poor planning. The starvation deaths, repeatedly in

Kalahandi, Orissa where couples are forced to sell off their children, for a few kilograms of grain, tells the tragic story. Our Public Distribution System today is catering only to the Economically Weaker Sections but a survey details that the grains, of far superior quality, are available in the open market for the same price.

The total callousness and irresponsible attitude of our government machinery, in ensuring purchase of decent quality food grains, at the government fixed price, needs to be investigated. The beneficiaries are the larger farmers, the rich and well off, who have political clout and who grease the palms of the officials to pass on substandard food grain to our state purchasing agencies.

Without imparting confidence to the smaller farmers, in getting a reasonable price for their produce, our agricultural production cannot reach the levels envisaged to feed our teeming millions. For this, we need brutally forthright officers who can blunt the efforts at corruption and motivate their task force into doing a proper job of the task allotted to them and for which they are handsomely paid for. It would also need the efforts of NGOs to properly motivate the smaller, illiterate farmers and ensure that they are not beguiled into selling their produce at inappropriate prices.

Other agencies like Doordarshan and All India Radio should repeatedly broadcast the framed guidelines to the rural masses so that they can stand up for their rights. This is what will give them confidence.

The proper utilization of our agricultural produce by State agencies will also ensure that there are no starvation deaths in our country even as millions of tones of food grain rots away in our State storage. This is the need of hour.

An Ideal Student

The very word: "Student" denotes a person fond of studies. But 'studies' do not mean just bookish knowledge, but a real knowledge of men, society, nature, mind, etc.

Such variegated knowledge can be obtained only by a person of strong mind and will, good heart and sound health. So, the very connotation of being an ideal student is one's keen interest in developing an all round personality.

By going into details, we can say that an ideal student has a thirst for knowledge. He has the curiosity to learn and understand new and new things about man and nature. He has a regular routine for doing everything. Thus, he is regular and punctual. He gets up early in the morning, takes regular exercise, has his bath and goes to his school or college in time. He devotes his time to studies whole-heartedly and is in the good books of his teachers whom he respects sincerely, as he respects his parents. He helps the weak students in their students and never makes fun of them. If others out do him, he accepts their superiority with humility. He may have a healthy competition with them, but he is never jealous of them. Similarly, he plays one or the other game, but with a sportsman's spirit.

An ideal student is very particular about his character and manners. He is truthful, honest and frank. He does not find fault with others but tries to get rid of his own drawbacks, if any. He has no evil habits like drinking, smoking, gambling etc. He is a great patriot and is ready to die for his country. He knows that by making himself strong in body and mind, he is also serving the national cause, because, as Emerson says, "Not gold but only men can make a nation great and strong."

An ideal student is very studious. He knows that an idle man's brain is the devil's workshop. He does the right thing at the right time. He believes in his own sincere effort. He does not believe in underhand methods. For instance, copying in the examination can never be his motto. He is in jet only a voracious reader and a good player but also a good speaker and writer. He believes in bringing constant efficiency in his work. He has a positive and an optimistic attitude towards life. Failures do not depress him, nor do successes turn his head. He has a balanced mind and personality.

Space Programme– Reasons and Benefits

Astronomy and Space Science is an ancient science researched in India right from early civilization. Details of the solar system, planets, stars and other phenomenon like eclipse and records of comets have been found in the Vedic times.

The modern branch of space research started with the setting up of the Indian Meterological Department at Colaba, Bombay (Mumbai) in the year 1823. The Calcutta (Kolkata) University started the study of space and ionosphere, located in the upper regions of our atmosphere, around the mid- 20's of the last century followed by higher studies in the field of astrophysics. This gained momentum in the 50's spreading to other centres over the country followed by the setting up of high power telescopes at the Madras (Chennai) and Kodaikanal observatories.

Modern space programme received an impetus with the leadership of Dr. Vikram Sarabhai and facilities developed at Thumba, near Thiruvananthapuram, Kerala for launching of space vehicles. This facilitated the two stage launch of a Sounding Rocket in 1969 and India was on its way.

Indian Space Research Organization functioning under the aegis of Department of Space, Government of India is the apex body for providing direction to our space programme in terms of scientific and administrative functioning. It is overall responsible for execution, planning and management of space related technology and applications. There are several units and auxiliary wings functioning in tandem with ISRO which are the SHAR centre at Sriharikota, the Vikram Sarabhai Centre at Thiruvananthapuram, the Space Application Centre at Ahmedabad, ISRO Satellite Centre located in Bengaluru etc.

The expenses incurred are quite mind-boggling but it has been found necessary for weather survey, geological mapping and survey, satellite communication and remote sensing. They are also of help in the research of atmosphere and meteorology. And for these we need indigenous technology for developing rockets and satellite to help in the research activities.

ISRO has successfully developed various types needed to reach different levels of the atmosphere and to be remote controlled to send back the necessary data. The range is wide from a rocket able to lift a 10 kgs payload to a height of 10 kilometres to the one capable of rising to more than 300 kilometres with a heavier pay load of about a 100 kgs.

Several launch vehicles have been successfully used by ISRO in the SLV series and the PCLV series which have resulted in our country being bracketed in the category of countries capable of launching Intermediate Range of Ballistic Missiles. The necessity of developing these IRB missiles was felt as Pakistan, our neighbour and enemy country was already into this with their Ghaurim Ghazanavi and HATF missiles tested and deployed against us. China has been covertly and overtly transporting the necessary knowhow to them over the decades. The developed countries of the Western hemisphere have been unduly pressuring India to ban its space programmes while they have not been able to restrain Pakistan.

We deserve kudos for being successful in our developments under a total ban on any supply of missile technology from any country at all whereas Pakistan had the advantage of dedicated help from China and North Korea. The development of this technology, although more expensive for us, was needed to ward of threat from our neighbours, right fully acting as a deterrent. The Vikram Sarabhai Space Centre was entrusted the task of the Augmented Satellite Launch Vehicle and the Polar Satellite Launch Vehicle, ASLV and PSLV, which they successfully did.

The first satellite developed and launched by us was the 'Aryabhatta' in April 1975, although it was out in orbit by a Soviet Cosmos Rocket from a Soviet cosmodrome. This marked the first step in competent satellite technology. A remote sensing satellite 'Bhaskara' followed in June 1977 again from the erstwhile USSR. This contained two TV cameras and three microwave radiometers to transmit remote sensing imagery. Bhaskara II followed in 1981 and was in use till recently for imageries. Other functions and experiments are still continuing.

The more versatile INSAT series was planned for domestic telecommunications, geological and meteorological surveys and direct television transmission, all over the country network for beaming rural programmes. Unfortunately the first in the series INSAT-1A launched in 1982 could not be fully activated initially. In needed the support of the multipurpose satellite

INSAT-1B launched in August 1983, to restore its operating capability. The use of the US space shuttle Challenger was instrumental for its launch.

The first experimental geostationary communication satellite INSAT-1C was launched in July 1988 from French Guyana. It was not indigenous and was assembled at the Ford aerospace. The purpose was to expand television and telephone capacities and collect metereological data. However, this satellite was not upto the demands made and had a very short span due to short circuit.

In the same year, 1988, there was the launch of the just Remote Sensing Satellite IRS-1a by a Soviet Rocket 'Vostok'. The satellite weighing nearly a tone was put in a Polar Sun Synchronous orbit at the height of more than 900 kilometre. There were three cameras installed with detectors based on charge coupled devices, providing four band data. Three of these are of viable nature and the fourth one nearly infra-red. The National Remote Sensing Agency at Hyderabad monitors the data and makes it available.

US help was again needed for the launch of INSAT-1D. The MeDonnel Douglas Corporation of USA blasted this off its Delta 4925 rocket successfully a long need felt after the failure of INSAT-1C. This has been of great help with its

C-Band transponders for public utilities and Government telecommunication transmission facilities. The S-B transponders are being utilized for television broadcast.

Then INSAT-1 series of satellites were quite a drain on our resources worth nearly Rs. 60 crore each and that too in foreign exchange. The INSAT-2 series were planned in 1990 with an estimated cost of Rs. 40 crore each. The experiment was to reduce the payload of each satellite and try to place two smaller ones in orbit, near each other and working in tandem. T he signals to be received and transmitted were to perpendicular to the other satellites. Five of the series were launched starting with INSAT-2A in July 1992 and ending with INSAT–2E in April 1999. The latter was a launch with minimum hassles and will remain operational for more then a decade. The vehicle carries 17 transponders with Intel Sat the global consortium cornering the bulk in lease.

The data is to be used mainly for communication and weather monitoring, specially advanced information on destructive storms. The other important purpose, which is beneficial to the Cable TV operator, is that most of the channels are using these for TV broadcast and the operator needs to align his dish antennae with them for maximum signals. ISRO took its first giant step towards commercial utility of its launches by launching three satellites at one go with the help of a single launch vehicle PSLV-C2 or the polar satellite launch vehicle. The three launched were, a massive one tonne Ocean Sat-1 of ours and two smaller ones from Germany and Korea. The feasibility was proved and we already have bookings from some developed countries for future launches.

Experiments on fitting cryogenic engines for the next generation of rockets the GSLV or Geosynchronous Satellite Launch Vehicle is at the final stage. A commercial wing of Antrix Corporation has been formed in line with the Western corporations. The sanctions were earlier to avoid this new competition from a third world country and stands exposed. The Western corporations will do the best to ensure that this venture is not a success and we should be prepared to tack them on. We are entering a new threshold and need to be dedicated and clear-eyed about our goal.

Women in Workplace

In the past decade a dramatic increase in the number of women participating in the labour force has taken place. Since early history and the ancient civilization of man, women have played a secondary role, in which women were and still are viewed as less then a man. A women's role in society was that of raising children, and duties surrounding the household. Many women today want and desire careers and a place in this world. They want to stand on their own two feet, to become self-sustaining individuals, independent and free from other individuals. The one thing that is clear is that women in all careers are striving to gain equality in the work force today.

The issues that have and still surround women and the workplace are many. For a long time women were at a disadvantage when it came to competing with men in the workplace. Women were not given the educational opportunities that men were, and women were stereotyped into certain jobs. Discrimination of women in the workplace has for years been feed by gender bias. Since the time when women entered the workforce they have been paid less than a man for doing the same job.

Although women in the workplace have had several odds stacked against them one thing remains clear, that women have and still do make a great contribution to the workplace. Through their determination, women have been a driving force in the enactment of laws to protect themselves and others in the workplace. These laws are not just for gender discrimination but also include discrimination based on martial status, pregnancy, race, disabilities, sexual preference, and age. Women now have the ability to break out of the gender roles that were created for them by society long ago.

One of the issues that has affected women in the workplace is that of stereotyping of women. Throughout history women have taken the role of housewife, mother, and nurturer. Women are stereotyped to stay at home and take care of the house and children. It has been their job to cook the meals, do the laundry, and manage the children's school activities. Even today, motherhood is still considered to be the primary role for women. Women that do not take on this role are still today thought of as selfish. Women that look to establish careers outside the home, for years, were thought of as being selfish and self-centered. Because women were viewed as homemakers they were often given jobs that were meaningless, and they were not thought of as managers or professionals.

Clearly, circumstances of family life have changed in the modern era. Large populations of women have, and will continue to join the workplace. Although this period of change has helped to shape the role of women today, women in corporate India is still oppressed. Even today, women are not treated the same as men. One area that clearly shows this oppression is the area of equal pay for equal jobs. The female labour force is seen as an inferior part of the work force. When looking at earnings and job distribution, a person could assume that women were in some way not as accomplished or competent as men. Yet a more in depth investigation would show that women are just as qualified as men.

Area in which women are at a disadvantaged in the workplace is through discrimination. Discrimination can be an uncomfortable situation for the women involved. There are two types of discrimination, indirect and direct, each affects women in a different way. Indirect discrimination might be a women being overlooked for a promotion, or an employee displaying inappropriate sexual material in the workplace.

Direct discrimination may include a women being discharged from her employment because she is pregnant, or being excluded from after work group events. There are laws that address direct discrimination, however people can find very slight ways of discriminating, making it hard to prove.

Another major area were women have been affected in the workplace is sexual harassment. Women working in low level jobs are often the targets of sexual harassment. Sexual harassment is very damaging to women, and the workplace. Most of the time the harassment goes unreported. Up until just a few years ago women had no recourse when confronted with such harassment by a boss or co-worker. This conduct has the purpose or effect of unreasonably interfering with an individual's work performance, or creates an intimidating, hostile or offensive working environment.

Another form of sexual harassment can be by men expressing their resentment and trying to reassert control when they view women as economic competitors. Sexual harassment is closely linked to sex discrimination. Sexual discrimination forces women into lower paying jobs, and sexual harassment helps keep them there. One thing is clear, whether the problem is sexual harassment or sexual discrimination the problem continues to exist in the workplace, reminding women of their vulnerability and creating tension that make their jobs more difficult.

In the last decade companies have turned their attention to some of these issues. There has been more training and education about women's issues, such as sexual harassment, in the workplace. Even though there is more corporate training for these issues, this training may not work, but educating people is a start. Women need to overcome the image that they are sensitive people, which let their emotions control their mind. They need to prove that they can think with their minds and not their hearts when it comes to business. No matter what sex a person is there will be times in life when the person is confronted with, and must defeat, a stereotype based on the person's sex.

Most people want to correct the unequal treatment of women in the workplace. One method that can be used to support equality would be to introduce federal legislation to guarantee equal pay for equal work. The logistical problems associated with this solution would be great. How would people measure the value of one person's work to another's? Who would decide this and how would it be implemented?

Our attitudes toward women in the workplace are slowly starting to change. More opportunities are appearing for women workers today then ever before. The unequal treatment of working women will take years to change, but change is occurring. This topic will remain until people treat and pay women equally, based upon their abilities and nothing else.

There have been many remedies introduced into the workplace that have tried to address the injustice toward women in the workplace. Although there have been many improvements for women in the workplace, there are still many inequalities for women when compared to men. Remedies are needed to secure women a fair, and equal role in the workplace. However, I do think that gender equality can be achieved. This change can only fully occur when we change the attitudes of every individual toward women. When we accomplish that then we can finally achieve gender equality in the workplace.

Nuclear Power

As time passes and our world becomes more technologically developed there is a greater need for energy sources. Most of the fuels we use today are not renewable e.g. oil and coal.

Nuclear Power is a source of energy which has many benefits. Nuclear energy is less expensive because it is based on uranium which is very accessible. With little amount of uranium a great amount of energy can be produced. It is a reliable source to rely on as there is significant amount of it on the Earth's crust.

One important advantage is that producing energy using Nuclear Power does not give off Greenhouse gases. Green house gases are gases like carbon dioxide and sulphur dioxide which are contributing to the Greenhouse effect or Global Warming. The biggest advantage of Nuclear Power is the discoveries made in Nuclear Medicine, such as cancer therapy, CAT scan and MRI machines and the use of irradiation of food to kill bacteria.

Nuclear Power has been used in the last hundred years for the manufacture of Nuclear Weapons like A-Bombs (atomic bombs) and H-Bombs (hydrogen bombs). Nuclear Weapons are weapons of mass destruction. A single weapon can be capable of destroying of seriously disabling an entire city. In the history of warfare Nuclear Weapons have been used on two occasions, both during the closing days of World War II in Hiroshima when a devise called 'Little Boy' was dropped and then three days later one in Nagasaki called 'Fat Man'.

It is a good idea to possess Nuclear Weapons if you are a 'Super Power'. If a country feels threatened it can rely on Nuclear Weapons to protect them from the enemy. Examples of 'Nuclear Super Powers' are USA, Russia, United Kingdom and France.

Nuclear Weapons have many disadvantages. The use of them can lead to a world crisis as every time a bomb explodes the lives of millions of people are affected and those close to the explosion are vaporised in a split second. Nuclear Weapons are very expensive to manufacture even though the uranium is accessible.

Nuclear Power has many disadvantages too. Nuclear plants are on of average 75% to 80% reliable. If an accident occurs, in USA for example, according to a 1982 study done by Sandia National Laboratories, it would result in deaths of thousands of people, latent cancers and the loss of billions of dollars.

We have all seen movies where whole cities have to be evacuated when a Nuclear Power plant is about to explode. That is fiction but can become reality.

One major disadvantage of Nuclear Power is that it makes variable amounts of radioactive waste. This waste is causing big problems for the world storage because of its irradiation. The nuclear waste has to be stored over a hundred years and the waste remains hot for thousands of years.

Some people say Nuclear energy is cheaper to make but this is not the entire truth. Since its beginnings, Nuclear Power has cost USA over 450 billion dollars nearly twice the cost of the Viet Nam war and the Apollo mission combined.

Although Nuclear Power has many disadvantages I think it is necessary as long as it is used for a good cause. The fossil fuels we are currently using for making energy are some day going to run out so we need other sources to rely on. If Nuclear Power is handled correctly the possibility of an accident is very rare. Each year about 50 000 people die due to the respiratory illnesses in America caused by the burning of coal. The chance of a nuclear accident that would cause that kind of damage to humans is like 1 in every 250 years.

I think Nuclear Power is a good substitute to burning fossil fuels for energy as it does not contribute to Global Warming.

Although I agree with the use of nuclear energy I do not agree with the manufacture of Nuclear Weapons. I think that any object or instrument manufactured for the destruction of humanity should be forbidden. Nuclear Weapons not only cause massive destruction, the money that countries invest for the manufacturing and testing of these weapons can be used to feed millions of poor people.

Cyber Terrorism

With the mushrooming growth of Information Technology applications in the critical functioning of various infrastructures, associated closely with appliance and our everyday life, the focus has been sharpened on the security of Critical Infrastructure Protection by nations around the world.

Common among such infrastructures are the essential services like electricity, telephone connectivity, vehicular and railway traffic control and gas/oil transportation. As such infrastructures are dependent more on IT, their vulnerability has increased manifold.

Today, with cyberspace becoming an easy medium for disturbance by hackers–both individual and state sponsored, as well as terrorist organizations whose main aim is to sabotage and disrupt facilities, high priority protection of such infrastructures are on the top of the agenda of the countries.

As a concept, Critical Infrastructure Protection or CIP was projected first in USA in 1996 by the then President Bill Clinton, as a result of a high level commission report. The report proved the susceptibility and necessity of taking a closer look at protection provided to high priority infrastructures. George Bush had set-up a special board after the September 11 attack, when he realised the urgency of the situation with New York practically paralyzed and vital systems sabotaged.

Most of the developed and developing nations all over the world have woken up-to the situation now and several countries like Canada, Sweden, Germany, Norway, Holland and Switzerland are falling in line with US initiatives. These are under a specially created wing under defense and intelligence ministries or a special task force has been created for the purpose. Some of these nations have multi-lateral agreements with other countries for sharing the resources. Although there is no global forum to tackle such issues but our country has an exclusive one to USA to fight the menace of CIP and counter Cyber Terrorism. But the European Union countries have a common federation.

Our country had earlier faced the problem with Pakistan backed defence hackers jamming our troop movement communication system giving false commands and creating a situation of uncertainty. Taking this as a small example, we need to set-up an action plan on a war-footing. The National Security Council is already in touch with several ministries like home, defence, communication, oil and natural gas, etc. to draw up plans. But our planning and implementation gap has always been unpardonably long. Instead of waiting for some incident and regretting later, a strong independent body directly under the Prime Minister should be set-up having implementation, intelligence and research functions.

Cyberspace surveillance is absolutely on top priority and a para-military force allotted for training in computer security, information security and communication security. They should also be trained to provide security to agencies developing critical software application besides personnel security as foreign intelligence agencies like ISI of Pakistan have always been targeting such staff and development bodies. The vulnerability of cyber attacks and the cascading effect of critical interdependent infrastructures falling prey to this menace need to be securitized. All such organizations need to coordinate their physical, satellite and cyber protection security to work in tandem and not separately.

We are a country which has already left its mark in the software world and our software world and our software prowess should be geared up for research and analysis. An emergency response strategy should be worked upon, to be activated in case of need. We have a very advanced set-up in Pune –Centre for Development of Advanced Computing (CDAC) which has successfully developed a high general purpose parallel computer by using off the self hardware and industry standard interface, the Param-9000, successor to Param-8000 and Param-8600. This setup should be made the modal agency and given charge for developing critical software to tackle cyber terrorism. The efficiency of this recommended organization has been proved by their latest Param-10000 which is now Asia's second largest computer and at contemporary levels with Super-Computers in USA.

The countries which faced the holocaust of the World War II and reduced to rubbles once again have risen like the Phoenix to the top of the list of developed nations. Look at Japan, Israel, Germany and their remarkable progress. It is only due to the inculcation of discipline in their blood. They have the natural sense of responsibility and they know their obligations to their nation. This results in discipline in every field of life. A visitor from the Third World countries stares aghast at the orderliness and neatness in developed countries. Trains run on time, essential services are of high standards, cleanliness is their motto, queuing up is an inherent trait, officials are polite and do their jobs.

Compare this with our country and we can understand where and why we are lagging behind. Is it the whip we need? How is it that the much maligned promulgation of 'Emergency' by a former Prime Minister transformed our nation, nationals and the bureaucracy into a disciplined, well-oiled task force?

A singular case may be cited. Once a journalist, from a leading newspaper of our country, asked an important leader in U.K., "We believe that discipline is in the very blood of your people". The leader smiled and shook his head in negativity, "No, it is not inherent. It is a cultivated quality. From family to society, from society to nation, it is a very long and arduous process. Efforts are made to let this quality of discipline flow like the blood in our nation's body!"

Corruption in India

Corruption is rampant in India. It is like a cancer that is eating away at the innards of the country. Government employees are some of the most corrupt people in India.

Of course, not all of them are corrupt but a good percentage of them take bribes from those who approach them to get something done. One reason for this is that government employees in most states are not paid good salaries and wages remain stagnant in public sector companies for years. As the cost of living increases, people find it hard to make ends meet and they resort to corruption to make extra income.

If you want to get a driving license or a ration card or a marriage certificate or a birth or death certificate, most probably you may have to grease someone's palm in the concerned office. There is corruption in every field. Political and electoral institutions are largely responsible for India being perceived as one of the most corrupt countries in the world. Corruption among the police force and judiciary has serious consequences for criminals go scot – free endangering society.

Corruption in the academic field means that merit is ignored and mediocrity exalted. Politicians embezzle public funds and take kickbacks. Corruption reigns even within the hallowed precincts of religious institutions. It makes a mockery of medical ethics in hospitals. The Satyam scandal blew the lid off the myth that India's IT sector is immune to such things.

In short, nothing is sacrosanct when it comes to this evil practice. If left unchecked, corruption spreads rapidly. It also makes people resigned to it and saps their will to fight it. They become pessimistic and soon they also begin to ignore the law. Corruption causes inefficiencies and diverts resources. The poor are most affected by corruption. Even PDS rations meant for the poor find their way into the open market.

India's rank slipped from 72 to 85 (out of 179 countries) in Transparency International's Corruption Perceptions Index. TI is the global barometer of corruption. In India, corruption exists in the form of bribes, tax evasion and exchange controls, embezzlement, etc. Corruption has many economic consequences.

It causes great loss to the exchequer, creates an unhealthy

climate for investment and increases the cost of government-subsidized services. It is not very easy to do business in India. Compared to China and other prosperous Asian nations, the average time taken to secure the clearances for a startup or to invoke bankruptcy is much greater in India.

Recently, the Right to Information Act was enacted by the UPA government. A UN development report termed it the most progressive legislation in the developed world. This Act has enabled the public to demand accountability from government institutions regarding processes. But the power of the Act has not been fully utilised because of low awareness.

One way to diminish corruption would be to increase pay scales of lower grade government employees. Also, there should be a carrot and stick policy to reward efficient people and punish corrupt ones. Increased transparency and vigilance is the need of the hour.

Wars–Destructive for Humanity

War is, without argument the worst collective experience of humanity. It has created new nations on the rubbles of destroyed cities and humans dead.

It involves mass killing without humane feelings even if short and swift. Our recent experience with Kargil, which was not even not even a full-fledged war, reopened the sordidness of military action.

Wars, when prolonged like the World Wars, result in human brutality, mass extermination of races and intolerable atrocities on innocent civilians. All rules are kept on the backburner and what matters is victory or defeat. The 21st Century has seen the development of weapons, controlled by computerized systems, with pin-point accuracy and a million-fold increase in powers of destruction compared to our previous wars.

Weapons and tactics have undergone total transformation in the last millennium but no deterrent has managed to quell human conflict. It may look totally different has managed to quell human conflict. It may look totally different for the war-mongers but not the common man it gives the same results – death and destruction. The totally of wars since 1945 right from Nagasaki and Hiroshima to Iraq and Afghanistan continue to grow without respite. The irony of the new millennium is that improvement in technology and scientific advancement have given us more options, leaving us with our major drawback, our primitive human failing – the fear of the other.

The core reasons for fighting wars are about proving superiority, hegemony, competition for dominating the region or the world and for economic survival. The recent wars, to preserve the efficacy of the democratic system, may be a phase which is temporary.

The US military historian and analyst Colonel Macgregor states this explicitly, "We did not fight Hitler just because he was a Nazi or the fight against Stalin was not because he was a Communist." Similarly the US ambassador to NATO asserted, "Our shared values of freedom, democracy, the rule of law, respect for human rights are themselves every bit as much worth depending as our territory". This may be applicable for the war on Iraq or Afghanistan but vital interests are of primary importance. Otherwise why has NATO kept allot from Kashmir, Africa, Chechenay or Algeria inspite of terrorism and absolute human suffering. Examples of Bosnia, Kosovo and East Timor are now exceptions but do raise our expectations for intervention in cases of upholding human rights.

The situation has drastically changed today with hand-held missiles capable of bringing down aircraft. The US faced this situations in Somalia and Afghanistan. Even very back in 1993, the US experienced the result of new weapons, in the hands of hurriedly formed mercenary and militia. The ragged, underfed and ill uniformed militia was capable of bringing down helicopters and kill marines, wrecking a super-power campaign in Somalia. The civil war in Somalia was further intensified due to their intervention. The bloodshed in Algeria continued in 1998 but the NATO and other super-powers including France just sat back and twiddled their thumbs.

Serbia also proved a point by creating a human crisis which could not be solved by the forces of NATO, It had to find its own solution to the problem. Intervention in Yugoslavia or Iraq has not been able to subdue the rulers there and even after carpet bombing and unleashing their might the NATO powers could not reach a conclusion.

From these results, it has been proved that self-imposed political limitations on the amount of force to be used, can simply leave problems unresolved. The future holds more terror with smaller States like North Korea going in for nuclear weapons and States like Pakistan passing on technology to other Islamic states. The day is not far off when Islamic militants will be able to get together a makeshift weapon. Major powers will be facing the paradox of yet more asymmetric warfare by small adversaries wielding outsize weapons capable of atomic explosions and chemical warfare.

India had this situation at Kargil when they faced a few hundred mercenaries, terrorists and Pakistani militia, entrenched at the heights. The result was that it took us 50 days of all out effort leaving is with 407 dead and 584 wounded, with six missing. It was only after the Air Force was put into substantial use that we succeeded in our efforts to recapture the god-forbidden heights.

Air campaigns alone today, can bring about drastic results and with precision air power alone serve as an effective and peacemaking lever. The surrender and demise of the Taliban Government in Afghanistan was activated by the non-stop aerial bombing by US fighter bombers. The terrain and the weather would have made any other mode a long drawn process with casualties shooting sky high.

Experts are of differing opinions on the strategy to be adopted in the face of threats from rogue States and fanatical groups like Islamic fundamentalists as well as peacekeeping tasks that stop short of full-fledged war. In today's context, arms proliferation has speeded up. 'The right computer chip in an adaptable missile aboard an off-shore trawler or a pick-up truck, makes a formidable weapon of mass destruction, launched by a small but implacable foe.'

The call by US today of a space shield and an anti-missile defence are prompted not by fear of a superpower like the erstwhile Soviet Union, but countries like Libya, Iraq, North Korea or terrorists who have caused havoc and destruction all over the world. The latter could not be cowed down even after near destruction of Afghanistan. All the US monitors and technology could not stop the 9/11 terror of the towers being destroyed. The pace of war between nuclear powers has receded, but these terror annihilations by groups. Can they be stopped? It's a different kind of war now, but as destructive or even more than earlier, for humanity.

The Age of Information Technology

This technological age is a highly revolutionary age and of all the technological revolutions the information technology has attained the peak of its growth.

This explosion in information technology was not foreseen some years ago, and all over the world information technology has helped spread of information from one place to another very, very quickly. Computers are the backbone of this information technology industry. The unexpected growth of information technology is one of the greatest developments in technology.

What is called 'computer literacy' is essential these days. In fact illiteracy has come to mean now-a-days the lack of knowledge of the operation of computers. Students will lag behind in the race of life if along with a degree in a subject they do not have knowledge of computer science. They should study computer science even if they have not opted for the course in school or college, for, the operation of a computer has become part and parcel of our everyday life. In fact, some graduates, who have not taken up computer science in college but study computer science outside their college, have got jobs.

Computers help us to pass on a piece of information from one end of the world to another in a few seconds. E-mails sent through computers are a source of the quickest transmission of messages.

Some years ago we had to communicate with our relative or friend in the USA, England or Japan only through letters, and it would take some days for the letters to reach our relative or friend. Now, computers have made the world a global village. For, we give messages to our relative or friend abroad through e-mails which take only some minutes or seconds to reach him or her. It is very easy; it is very thrilling to work with a computer. Computer games are a source of great excitement to the children.

I have joined the computer science course in my school. Learning the basics of the computer science will help me to join the computer science degree course in a college. If I get a degree in the computer science it will help me seek a job in a multinational software engineering company where I can get good salary.

The software engineering field is fast expanding. The Indian software engineers are sought after abroad as they are found to be hard-working and efficient. Hundreds of young software engineers work in foreign companies and they are paid well.

Once posting of accounts in ledgers and pass books in banks was done manually and it had to be checked by an officer and signed. Now-a-days, computers are used in banks for posting of accounts and this has made the bank operations quite easy. Computers are reliable for their accuracy.

I have a computer at home and it is convenient for me to send e-mails to my brother and sister in the U.K. as often as possible.

The benefits of information technology have not reached the rural areas. First the Government and the educational institutions should take efforts in making the villagers literate and then they should be made aware of the benefits of information technology.

Cultural Unity of India

India is a well-marked geographical unit. It is big in size and dimensions. It is more like a continent than a country. It is as large as Europe without Russia and about twenty times the area of Great Britain.

In its vastness are found such varied physical features and social conditions that India has aptly been described as the epitome of the world. It is a land of varied diversity. It is one of the most ancient cultures of the world.

India is characterized to be country with the one in many, the individual in the aggregate, the simple in the composite. With them the whole is lost in the parts. The millions of people have different faiths and cults and observe different customs and rites. There are endless diversities in India. Despite, culturally India is one and whole.

The diverzity itself far from being a damaging cause of disunity and weakness. It is a fertile source of strength and wealth. It is fundamentally tolerant and absorbing. This nature of Indian culture has helped to keep it alive.

The civilization of India has many features. It differentiates it from other regions of the world. But these attributes are common to the whole country. Indian culture is dynamic and flexible. It has survived many foreign invasions due to its great power of assimilation.

Even the early Indian history shows that the political consciousness of the people has from the very early times, grasped the whole of India as a unit. They assimilated the entire area as theatre of its activities. India is not a mere geographical expression, nor is it a mere collection of separate people, traditions and conventions. It is much more than this. The best proof lies in the fact that Indian history has quickened into life.

India has many races, castes, sub-castes, and communities. But the heart of India is one. We are all heirs to a common and rich culture. Our cultural heritage consists of our art and literature as they flourished centuries ago. Our cultural heritage serves as a bond of unity between people of different faiths and creeds. India has over one hundred and fifty dialects and twenty-two recognized regional languages, but Hindi like English, has come to stay as the lingua franca of our nation. From Kashmir to Kanyakumari and from Mumbai to Nagaland, Hindi is now understood by the masses. It is recognized as the national language of India. It is a general medium of communication.

India has a rich cultural heritage. We are inheritors to several great treasures in the fields of music, fine arts, dance, drama, theatre and sculpture. Our sages and seers have left behind a tradition of piety, penance, spiritual greatness, conquest of passion, etc. Our scriptures are the storehouses of spiritual wisdom. Our saints and rishis aspired to the realization of the infinite. We have inherited great spiritual values. It is quite contrary to the materialist west. The west has a lot to learn from India. Now more and more people in the United States and Europe are turning to the Indian way of life, 'Indian yogis and maharishis, musicians and spiritual leaders, have all attracted them in a big way. The west is fast inclining towards our spiritual values. They include meditation and contemplation, charity and love, universal brotherhood and fear of God, piety and unselfishness, control of passions and peace of mind.

Our cultural unity is further exemplified by the temples of the South, the caves of the Khajuraho, Ajanta and Ellora, which are shining examples of India's proficiency in sculpture and architecture. Our music has come to enjoy worldwide popularity. We should preserve our cultural unity.

Importance of Cleanliness

The high value attached to cleanliness is expressed by the proverb which says that "Cleanliness is next to Godliness." Indeed, in some religions, cleanliness is regarded as a part of godliness and is prescribed as a religious duty.

In the law of Moses the priests were required to wash their persons and their clothes, when they had to appear before God, and the tradition of the Jewish elders rigorously enforced the washing of hands before meals. Mahomet prescribed frequent ablutions which, if water could not be had, were to be performed with sand.

Such ordinances are in part due to the recognition of the close connection between personal cleanliness and moral goodness. It is not without reason that white raiment and ceremonial ablutions have been chosen as the symbols of purity of soul that is expected of the priest and his congregation, when engaged in the solemn worship of God.

Even in our ordinary everyday life we see that a dirty man in dirty clothes is apt to lose that feeling of self-respect, which is one of the best safeguards against dishonesty and vice.

Another reason why the founders of religions prescribed frequent ablutions, was because they recognised the immense importance of cleanliness from a sanitary point of view. Dirt is known to be a fertile propagator of disease.

The germs of cholera and other deadly plagues are carried through the air with the dust that is seldom wanting under a tropical sun. The best means of avoiding infection is continual washing, which prevents those germs from remaining long on the body.

Unfortunately immunity from disease cannot be secured by being clean oneself. A scrupulously clean person may catch disease from the dirty persons with whom he comes into contact. Therefore the rich and intelligent must, in their own interests, provide their poorer neighbours with the means of keeping themselves clean.

Many benevolent rich men have done good service to the community in which they live by providing in crowded quarters of great cities fountains, from which the poor can get abundant supplies of water.

When water is scarce, and not to be obtained near their doors, the poor cannot afford the time necessary to get it from a distance, and remain dirty, to the great danger, not only of themselves, but also of their richer neighbours. This is the chief reason why the poor quarters of great cities are often hot-beds of disease.

The Municipal Corporation of Greater Mumbai, for example, fully recognizes the importance of these considerations, and has at an immense cost provided an abundant water-supply for this city.

So that there may be plenty of water not only for drinking purposes, but also to water the streets, and wash the houses, the persons, and the clothes of all the inhabitants.

Our Duties to the Poor

Many successful people in easy circumstances refuse to admit that they have any duties to the poor. They agree with Tennyson's "Northern Farmer" when he said, "The poor in a lump is bad." They comfort themselves with the belief that all poverty is due to laziness, drink, or stupidity, and is, therefore, the fault of the poor themselves.

Even if this were true, we should still have a duty to the poor; for it is the duty of the wise, the strong, the industrious and the virtuous, to help the weak, the idle, the foolish and the vicious, to change their mode of life.

But it is not true; at any rate it is only a part of the truth. For in modern civilisation, a great deal of the terrible poverty that exists is not due to any fault of the poor themselves, but to the organization of society, for which the individual poor are not responsible. Whether a man is born rich or poor is a matter of chance. Many of the rich have simply inherited their wealth, and have in no way earned it; and many of the poor have in like manner inherited their poverty, and have in no way deserved it.

It matters not how idle and worthless the rich man is: he remains rich; and similarly it matters not how industrious and sober and able a poor man is, for under present conditions he is too often doomed to a life of poverty.

Leaving aside, therefore, cases of poverty that are really due to idleness or vice, there is a large mass of poverty for which the modern social organization is responsible. These poor are therefore a legitimate burden on their more fortunate rich brothers, whose duty it is to relieve them in their distress.

Usually, the duty of the rich to the poor is summed up in the word almsgiving, or charity. It certainly is the duty of those who have to give of their abundance to those who have not, according to their needs.

But indiscriminate almsgiving, and even organized charity, is no solution of the problem of poverty; and the mere giving of money to the poor does not relieve a rich man of all further responsibility.

Nor is it enough to throw all the responsibility of the poor on the State. In England, the Government provides workhouses for the old people who are past work, for orphans, and even for able-bodied men out of employment.

But in order to discourage pauperism, these work-houses have to be made so undesirable that no poor people will willingly resort to them until they are forced to do so.

The poor require something more than money. They want intelligent sympathy; they want moral help, which no money can buy; they want to be treated as human brothers, and not as creatures of another race, and as dirt under our feet.

To give these things to the poor requires a larger heart, a broader mind, and more personal sacrifice, than most rich people are prepared to give. Yet we shall never be able to relieve the poor in any real way until we can give them our hearts as well as our money.

Finally, the chief duty of the rich is to so reorganize society that no man need be poor if he is industrious, sober and honest. This is a very difficult and complicated problem, which cannot be solved by any simple measures; but if a nation as a whole is resolved to abolish all poverty that is not due to individual vice and idleness, it will be able to find a way.

National Flag: Status and Symbol

There are certain moments in the cultural and political life of a nation when the national flag comes into prominence. Every Indian is aware that the Prime Minister unfurls the national tricolour from the ramparts of the Red Fort every

Independence Day on August 15 and indeed the observance of January 26th as Republic Day goes back to 31 December, 1929, when Jawaharlal Nehru hoisted the flag of the Indian National Congress, gave a call for *purna swaraj* and asked people to observe January 26 as Independence Day. The honoured dead are honoured with the flag and that if the national flag is attendant upon the birth of a nation, it equally accompanies in death those whose lives are construed as being symbolic of the nation.

Along with the national anthem, the national flag is supremely and specially iconic of the nation-state. It is understood that the honour and integrity of the nation are captured by the flag and as the history of every country shows, the national flag is uniquely capable of enlisting the aid of citizens, giving rise to sentiments of nationalism and evoking the supreme sacrifice of death: in every respect, the national flag commands, not merely our respect, but our allegiance. When the then Miss Universe, Sushmita Sen, was taken on a triumphant parade through the streets of Delhi, the manner in which her carriage displayed the national flag was found to be offensive. Attached to the back of her carriage, in direct defiance of the regulations stipulated in the *Flag Code-India*, the national flag appeared to have been compromised and demeaned, indeed, it appeared as though Sushmita Sen had rendered it into an item of consumption. Though Sen could, under the laws of the land, have faced fines and imprisonment, her own iconic significance, as the reigning beauty queen of the world and as a supposed paean to the glory of modern Indian womanhood, was scarcely to be underestimated and was shown at that moment to be hardly less than the iconic significance attached to the flag.

The flag has once again come into the news. In a highly significant ruling on September 21st, the Delhi High Court directed that the *Flag Code-India*, which governs the use and display of the National Flag, could not be so interpreted as to prevent an ordinary citizen of India from flying in a respectful manner the National Flag from the premises of his or her business or residence. In any case, the Flag Code, ruled the Court, was not to be construed as law and its contravention could not be enforced unless, of course, such contravention came within the purview of either the Emblem Act or the Prevention of Insult to National Honour Act.

Most Indians can scarcely have been aware that they were forbidden, apparently under pain of punishment, to fly the national flag from the premises of their residential or office buildings and it is just as unlikely that the proverbial 'man on the street' will view the judgement of the Delhi High Court as of any consequence to him. But this is no small victory for the Indian citizen, when we consider that a very significant chapter of the history of the independence movement was woven around the hard-won struggle of Indians to fly the flag of their choice. The present flag is, to a considerable degree and certainly in essence, the flag to whose design none other than Mahatma Gandhi lent his hand and which the Congress was to adopt in 1921. Writing for *Young India* on 13 April 1921, two years after the massacre at Jallianwala Bagh, Gandhi observed that the red in the flag represented Hindus, the green stood for Muslims and that the white represented all other faiths, the spinning wheel in the middle of the flag pointed to the oppressed condition of every Indian, just as it evoked the possibility of rejuvenating every Indian household. Gandhi did not think that the matter of the national flag trifling, as he was to put it, "A flag is a necessity for all nations. Millions have died for it. It is no doubt a kind of idolatry which it would be a sin to destroy." If the Union Jack could evoke immeasurably strong sentiments in English breasts, was it not necessary that all Indians "recognize a common flag to live and to die for"?

Gandhi's flag, as it was known to English officials, was with some modifications formally adopted by the Congress in 1931 as the National Flag and this flag in turn became the basis, with the substitution of the wheel on the capital of Asoka's Sarnath Pillar for the *charkha*, for the National Flag chosen by the Constituent Assembly in July 1947. In the meantime, between 1921 and 1947, a war of attrition developed between Indian nationalists and government officials over the right to fly the Gandhi or Congress flag. Indian nationalists found that hoisting the flag invariably attracted the wrath and often the vengeance, of British officials and usually the flag was ordered to be brought down.

Only once, at Bhagalpur in 1923, did the district official assent to a rare compromise, when he consented to have the Congress flag flown alongside the Union Jack, albeit at a lower height! This invited the reprimand of the Government of India and the British Cabinet, who wished to make it clear 'that 'in no circumstances should the Swaraj or Gandhi Flag be flown in conjunction with even below the Union Jack'. The more usual response was to have men and boys who defiantly carried the Congress Flag whipped and during the civil disobedience movement of 1930-33, boys as young as 8 years old were given 10-30 stripes each for this purported offence. A six-month long 'Flag Satyagraha' in Nagpur in 1923, in which a good part of the national leadership participated, led to the withdrawal of prohibitory orders on the use of the Congress Flag.

Thus, when we consider the arduous effort with which Indians established their right to fly their flag, it is all the more extraordinary, disturbing and deplorable that, in independent India, the state should have arrogated this right to itself and turned it into a privilege. It is fitting that the judiciary should now have restored this fundamental right to Indian citizens.

Indian Economy: Adopting New Approach

After independence, India chartered a path of economic development based on mixed economy, building a new industrial structure around the public sector and a closely monitored, regulated and controlled system where government played the role of licenser in the process of building industry.

There were few hiccups in between. In the late 70s Mrs. Indira Gandhi brought in small doses of liberalization. In the mid 80's Rajiv Gandhi did likewise but the real change came in 1991 when economic crises were looming large on the horizon.

India's economy could be termed as a developing economy which is characterized by the co-existence, in greater or lesser degree, of utilized or unutilized manpower on the one hand and of unexploited and exploited natural resources on the other.

A developing economy bears the common features of technological backwardness at low per capita income coupled by widespread poverty, heavy population pressure, low grade productivity, high unemployment, low level utilization of country's natural resources, rigid social structure, pre-dominance of old beliefs, lack of opportunity for capital formation, pre-dominance of agriculture and scanty participation in international trade etc.

But all this is amidst a possibility of economic development, small pockets of high rates of economic growth and affluence.

It is gain saying truth what the world economy has experienced that colonization directly lead to the exploitation of the colonized country by the colonial rulers.

Colonization is also a factor for the underdevelopment of a country's economy. India was a victim of the colonial feature of economic exploitation for more than hundred years.

The British colonial exploitation in India can be broadly divided in three periods. They are *(i)* the period of merchandised capital, *(ii)* the period of industrial capital which leads to the drain of Indian wealth for the interest of British industry and *(iii)* the period of financial capital.

During British period foreign capital flowed into India. However, in real terms those capitals were not according to the proper needs of Indians and directly helped the capital growth of the British.

The overall impact of British rule in Indian economy can be summed up as stagnation of per capita income ever a long period of time, high priority to the traditional method of agricultural activities, repeated famines and acute poverty of handicrafts and traditional village industries defective land holding and erroneous implementation of zamindari practices etc.

The basic aim of British administration in India was to transform Indian subcontinent as a consumer market for British furnished goods, Technological up-gradation and development of infrastructure as well as social infrastructure were negligible.

During the independence Indian economy had almost all

the features of an underdeveloped economy. In the last fifty years of self-rule, a lot of policy initiative has been taken up by the government of India to upgrade the economic base of the country.

Still Indian economy is gripped by poverty, population explosion, backwardness both in agriculture and industry, low grade technological development, high unemployment and wide difference between the high and low income levels. Now in India incidence of poverty is coexisting with sophisticated nuclear technology.

The policy measures taken within the last five decades metamorphosed Indian economy to break the stagnant per capita income to achieve self sufficiency in food grain production.

Indian economy is a unique blend of public and private sector otherwise known as a mixed economy. It is also a dualistic economy both modern industry and traditional agricultural activities exist side by side.

The mandatory economic rights which the Constitution promises are *(i)* equality of opportunity unemployment or appointment to any office irrespective of race, caste and sex, *(ii)* all the citizens of India shall have property or carry on any occupation, trade or business, *(iii)* right to acquire private property by the state with compensation paid under the procedure established by law, *(iv)* ban on begging, child labour and trafficking of human beings.

The federal economic structure of India includes the central government and the state government within a unitary system. Demarcations of responsibilities are divided between the central and state governments. However, the residuary power is vested with the central government.

Besides finance commission, other economic commissions are set-up by the central government time to time to look after the parity of resources distribution among the states. Annual budgets (both general and railway) and five year plans aye the backbone of India's economic policy initiatives.

Indian Economy since Independence– After India's independence long spell of stagnation was broken with the introduction of economic planning. Since 1950s net national product at factor cost had arisen from Rs. 40,454 crore to 11,224 crore in 1999-2000.

The growth of national income was 3.8 per cent. India's per capita income has been running since 1950-51. India's per capita income at current price is Rs. 66,119.

Apart from the growth in quantitative terms, there have been significant changes in India's economic structure since independence. During the second plan priority was acceded to capital intensive manufacturing units. These industries now account for more than fifty percent of the industrial production. The transport system in India over the past four decades has grown both in terms of capacity and modernisation. Then road network is one of the largest in the world as a result of spectacular development of roads under various lanes.

The total road length comprising national high ways state high ways and other road accounted for 24.66 lakhs km in 1996-97 progress of shipping, railways and civil aviation has equally been impressive.

Though the country is presently facing an energy crisis but this sector has also gained much in terms of production. Similarly irrigation facilities in the country have increased raising irrigated area.

Since independence significant reformation has taken place in the banking and financial sector of India. The process of nationalization was initiated after independence.

First the Reserve Bank was nationalized in 1949, thereafter in 1995 the Imperial Bank of India, a leading commercial bank of that time, was nationalized and renamed the State Bank of India.

In 1969, fourteen big commercial banks were nationalized. This act of government undermined the control of big capitalists on the finance capital.

From the above argument we can conclude that the Indian economy is no longer caught in low level equilibrium trap.

Importance of Games

The aim of education is the overall development of the personality of man. It means the development of not only the mind but also the body. Games keep the body fit. Swami Vivekanand was of the view that only a healthy mind can realize God. But a healthy mind can dwell only in a healthy body. For keeping a body healthy, games are indispensable. For this reason Swami Vivekanand had advised that all young men and women should play games. People who have developed the habit of playing games regularly can maintain good health. Games help to build a muscular body .They include sound sleep which is a sign of good health. Therefore, games are food for the body as knowledge is food for the mind. In fact, all work and no play make Jack a dull boy. Everybody likes games because these keep them physically fit and mentally alert.

Games help us to keep our body active and vigorous. They instill in us the spirit of adventure. They enable us to face dangers boldly. When a person plays games, his circulation of blood increases and his digestive system improves. He does not fall prey to any disease. Games inculcate in us the spirit of sportsmanship. They also teach us courage and perseverance.

Games foster the qualities of fairplay. Good players maintain equanimity in the event of victory or defeat. They also teach us a sense of discipline. A disciplined team has a greater chance of winning a match than a team which lacks discipline. Discipline is not only essential for the progress of an individual but also necessary for the development of a nation. Only a disciplined nation can hope to progress and prosper.

Games provide us with recreation and enjoyment. They refresh our mind and activate our body. They enable us to divert our mind from the daily routine of life. When we play games, we forget all our worries and anxieties.

A player respects the rules of the game he plays. He thus becomes a man of principles. Games enable him to follow other virtues like honesty, integrity and fairplay.

Games are very essential for students. The students of today are the citizens of tomorrow. If the students play games, they can learn the good things of life. They can lead a disciplined life. They can develop the virtues of patriotism and loyalty to the nation.

It is very disappointing that our players rarely win medals at the Olympic Games. Even players from small countries like South Korea, Cuba, Romania, etc. are able to win a large number of medals. We are far behind other countries in a number of games. One cannot resist the impression that in our country games are not given the importance that they deserve. We held the Ninth Asian games in Delhi in 1982. But we have not held a single Olympiad in our country so far. However, we shall be hosting the 19th Commonwealth Games in 2010.

It is, therefore, necessary that our Government should evolve a long term national sports policy. The students should be taught the advantages of games in the school itself. They should be given incentives for playing games regularly. Training facilities for various games should be upgraded and expanded. The existing system of selection of players for various meets and events should be streamlined unless we take these and other measures to popularise games, we cannot hope to bag medals at international sports events and Olympiads.

Various games and sports should also be popularised and encouraged in the rural areas of our country because nearly 72.2 per cent of the total population of our country lives in the villages. By holding games and sports in villages we can produce many sportsmen of an international level because villagers possess better health than city-dwellers. Possession of good health is a very important asset for the players and the sportsmen who aim at winning gold medals at international events and the Olympics.

In other countries of Europe and America and even in Asian countries like China, Japan and South Korea, games and sports are promoted in a big way. Therefore, we see that their players and sportsmen win a lot of gold medals in the international games and Olympics. It is due to the fact that sportsmen and sportswomen of these countries are given honour and big monetary incentives to encourage them to show feats of excellence and win gold medals.

To encourage the Indian players and sportsmen and sportswomen, our Government should also give them suitable monetary and other rewards like scholarships, promotion in service, preference in recruitment etc. so that they can also come upto the international standards and win gold medals for their country in the international games and Olympics.

Good Manners

Good manners play a very important role in the life of boys and girls. Though good manners are a very valuable possession for developing social relations, yet they cost nothing. They help a person to win friends. The social standing of a man is judged by the manners he possesses. Polished and polite manners create a healthy impact.

Good manners go a long way in making a person cultured and civilised. A man without good manners remains a savage. Normally good manners are inherited from parents. But these can also be learnt from others. It is, therefore, essential that all children are taught good manners from the childhood itself. Ill-mannered children bring disgrace to their worthy parents.

Children with good manners are liked by one and all. They are appreciated even by strangers. All round development of a child is possible only if a child is groomed in good manners. Therefore, the public schools lay great emphasis on the cultivation of good manners in their students. It is no exaggeration to say that a man without manners is an animal.

If a person is well-dressed it does not mean that he must be possessing good manners as well. We find that more often than not, even good-looking children lack good manners. The moment such children speak, they expose themselves. It is a matter of regret that some parents go on meeting the demands of their children but do not care to teach them good manners. These parents spoil them but when such children bring a bad name to them, they repent. But by then, it is too late. Therefore, if we want that our children should possess good manners and behave well, we must catch them young.

Courtesy and politeness is the key to good manners. Biographies of great men can also help us in learning good manners. The use of polite words like "Sorry", "Please", "Thank you", "Beg your pardon", "Sir" etc. creates a healthy impact on the minds of others. No doubt these are little words but if they are spoken at the right moment and in a soft and sweet voice, they are bound to work wonders. Even if we have to say "No" to someone, we should say so in a polite manner so that his feelings are not hurt.

Good manners not only demand courtesy and politeness but also respect for the feelings and opinions of other people. We should not criticise others for holding views different from us. We should avoid acrimonious discussions at social gatherings. They help no one. We should also steer clear of heated discussions on controversial and sensitive political issues to avoid bad blood with others. We should not ridicule a blind or a lame person. It shows bail manners.

We should be considerate to elders, ladies, children and sick persons while travelling in a bus or train, we should always offer them a seat. It is a pity that in buses, we sometimes find men occupying even the seats reserved for ladies. We should help an old lady or a blind person to cross the road safely. We should not talk loudly or shout at others.

While riding in a car or a scooter, we should not blow the horn unnecessarily especially near a hospital, school or a library/ we should not pluck a flower from any public garden. Flowers are meant to please our eyes and not to be plucked. If we go on talking to others but do not listen to what they have to say, it is a sign of bad manners. While I coughing or sneezing we should always cover our mouth with a handkerchief. We should not throw away banana skins on the roads. Someone might slip and sustain an injury. Similarly, the habit of writing obscene things on the walls or on books smacks of bad manners.

We should regard a foreigner as our most honoured guest. Whenever he needs our assistance, we should extend it to him. We should not jeer at him. Certain unscrupulous elements try to cheat foreigners of their money and belongings. This spoils the image of our country and its people in the eyes of the world.

While waiting for a bus, we should always stand in a queue. We should not try to break the queue even when we are in a hurry. All public property belongs to the nation. We should not damage it under any circumstances. These days, political parties have made the act of damaging public property like buses, trains, bridges, etc. a political weapon to press their demands or to air their grievances. This tendency needs to be curbed. We must treat public property as our own.

All great men are humble. They do not brag about their achievements. We should be happy over the achievements of others and not be jealous. If we know these people, we should congratulate them on their achievements. Criticizing a person behind his back is not good manners.

A well-mannered person is always the centre of attraction. He is loved and respected by all. Good manners bring joy and success in his life. He becomes a gem among his fellow men. We should acquire good manners and enrich our personality.

Fashion

Every one should try to have some leisure and make the best use of it by taking to some good hobby or the other. Great caution should be exercised; in choosing a hobby. We should choose a hobby which recoups our energy and provides relaxation and recreation.

Young people all over the world are becoming more and more fashion conscious. Young students, whether boys or girls, are crazy about it they want to look smart and beautiful by wearing dresses of the latest designs.

In order to boost the sales of their dresses, leading cloth mills and dressmaking firms engage reputed fashion designers and beautiful models. Fashion parades and shows are held in big five star hotels to exhibit the latest dresses.

Fashion is no longer the monopoly of women. Even men have great fancy for it. In fact, the latest uni-sex dresses like shirts and jeans can be worn both by the girls and the boys.

Today, the biggest centres of the latest fashions in the world are Paris, London, Hollywood and New York. In India, Mumbai, Delhi, Chandigarh, Lucknow, Jaipur, Shimla etc. have become centres of high fashion. Students generally try to copy fashions from films.

Fashion has permeated all spheres of our life. It is followed not only in clothes but also in hair-styles, shoes, etiquette or manners. Some people are content to wear fashionable clothes. Others go in for fashionable hair-styles. Still others adopt the latest trend in their speech and manner. All these people want to look impressive and attract the attention of others. They want to look different in the eyes of others.

Fashion is neither stable nor eternal. It is ever-changing. The change in fashion takes place so fast that people sometimes find it very difficult to catch up with it.

Students in India also have become quite fashion conscious.

In a college campus, one can see both girls and boys wearing all types of clothes. Girls wear whatever their favourite heroines wear. Boys try to emulate their favourite heroes.

Fashion knows no frontiers. It travels across countries very fast. When students in India see latest foreign films from Hollywood, they adopt the latest fashions from these films. They even imitate the way of life, speech, manners, actions, clothes, hair-styles of their favourite foreign actors and actresses.

Some students spend a lot of money and devote considerable time on their make-up. They neglect their studies. Their books gather dust. These students hardly realise that by neglecting their studies, they are ruining their own career. Students often seem to suffer from a mistaken notion that fashion means wearing clothes and other costly items like jewellery, etc. The fact is that sometimes expensive clothes and heavy make-up may prove counterproductive. It may even have a negative effect on one's personality. Some people look smarter in simple clothes than in expensive clothes. As the old saying goes, beauty needs no ornaments. In fact simplicity is the best fashion.

If students pursue fashion at the cost of their education, they will be left behind in their studies. This will spoil their prospects of a bright future. If they want to be successful in life, their motto should not be fashion but 'simple living and high thinking'.

Unfortunately, college boys and girls have started regarding even smoking as a fashion. One can see a number of boys and girls sitting in college restaurants and enjoying a smoke. Those who have costly brands of cigarette packets and imported cigarette lighters feel proud. Some students go to the extent of taking intoxicating drugs like 'heroin', LSD, Hashish, Marijuana, etc.

Drinking is also considered as a symbol of modern society and high fashion. These habits adversely affect the health of students. A conscious effort should be made both by the teachers and parents to dissuade their children from falling prey to these anti-social habits in the name of fashion.

No doubt fashion spreads like wild fire especially when fashion critics hail any new design as ultra modern. Slowly a fashion percolates first to the middle- class families and then to the poor strata of society. Once it becomes common, it loses its novelty. Fashion conscious boys and girls then look out for something else which is new and exclusive. But "fashion" should not be given wide meaning so as to include everything which is being followed in western countries. Due respect should be paid to one's native country's way of living also.

Whether the influence of western culture is a boon or a curse to the Indian youth, is a controversial topic. No culture is good or bad. After all, every culture is an educative refinement, a product of an era. It is the understanding of a culture and methods of pursuing it that can make it good or bad in the eyes of other people. Thus, it cannot be concluded that every western influence is harmful. Indian youth, instead of following the west blindly, should try to grasp the very essence of western culture and help it in enriching his own. Only then can true development take place.

Cinema–Its Uses and Abuses

Cinema is one of the most important inventions of modern science. The invention was made by Thomas Edison, a famous American scientist. Came is an effective medium for education and recreation. It plays a crucial role social, political, educational and moral life. It has come to occupy an import place in our life. Cinema attracts young boys and girls the most.

Nowadays, one can see a movie either on one's television set or at a cinema house. Students are always eager to see movies. Cinema halls draw huge crowds in their noon shows because a number of students see movies in these shows by missing their classes. The cinema halls also attract a great rusk of people on Saturdays and Sundays, when most of the offices are closed.

Feature films are being produced in India since 1912-13. While R.G. Torney along with N.G. Chitre made Pundalik in 1912, Dhundiraj Govind Phalke produced Raja Harishchandra in 1913. The era of silent films was overtaken by the talkie era in 1931 when Ardeshir Irani produced Alam Ara, though silent movies continued to be produced till 1934.

India leads the world in the annual output of feature films. These figures go to prove that cinema has become very popular in India. It has become a part and parcel of our life. Mumbai, Kolkata and Chennai are the most important centres of film production.

Films can be exhibited in India only after they have been certified by the Central Board of Film Certification. The Board, set-up under the Cinematograph Act, 1952 consists of a chairman and a minimum of 12 and a maximum of 26 members. The headquarters of the Board are at Mumbai.

Indian films are not only popular in India but also popular among many countries of South-East Asia and West Asia. They are also popular in Russia. The export of Indian feature films is channelised through the National Film. I Development Corporation the National Film Development Corporation (NFDC) is the central agency to promote good cinema in the country. It was set-up on 11 April, 1980 with the amalgamation of the erstwhile Film Finance Corporation and Indian Motion Picture Export Corporation.

The Indian film industry is a source of employment to many people. The cinema is a very economical source of entertainment for the common people. Any person can buy a ticket for a few rupees and see a movie at any cinema house. Cinema helps us to escape, for a while, from the worries and anxieties of life. It relieves us of tension. It provides us relaxation. It is for this reason that in a cinema-hall, we always find a cross-section of people-executives and workers, rich and poor, young and old, boys and girls, etc.

Cinema is a great source of education. It enlarges the frontiers of our knowledge. We can know about the culture, clothes, language, customs, etc. of people of other countries by seeing foreign films in India or seeing Indian films which have scenes shot in foreign countries. It saves us the botheration of physically visiting these countries. Documentary films also increase our knowledge. We can watch the scenes of different cities and countries while sitting in the comfort of cinema halls.

In a backward country like India, cinema can be a great source of education. We can gain knowledge of political, social and economic problems of our country. If educational films are produced, students of schools and colleges can benefit a lot in their studies. The students of today are the citizens of tomorrow. By showing them good movies, we can build the character of students and broaden their outlook. Cinema leaves a permanent and a deep impression on the minds of the people especially the young ones. It is, therefore, imperative that only good pictures are shown to our young students.

Cinema can be instrumental in bringing about much needed social reforms in our society. Social films can show the evils of untouchability, dowry, and child marriage, drinking, drug addiction, smoking, etc. and exhort the people to give up these evils in their own interest. Communalism raises its ugly head time and again in many parts of the country. Cinema can highlight the fact that communalism poses the greatest danger to the unity of the country. It can promote national integration. Cinema can also teach people to be law-abiding, to keep the environment clean, and to fight against diseases.

But films can also cause a lot of harm if they are made with an eye on the box office without bothering about the social content of these films. Unfortunately, most of the films being produced in Mumbai and other centres ire full of violence, nude scenes, rape scenes, cabaret dances, etc. They deliberately inject scenes of sex and violence in films and thus contaminate the social atmosphere of the society. If people are exposed to sex and violence all the time, they may be psychologically conditioned to accept them i routine facts of life, which in fact goes against the aims for which films are tide, that is, to bring unity and harmony among the people. Such films pollute ie minds of young boys and girls. Such filthy films create every bad impression the minds of young students who can easily go astray.

Similarly, films depicting sordid events like murders, robbery, theft, cheating, leave an adverse influence on the minds of the youth of our country. By seeing such films, young boys and girls develop criminal tendencies in the life. These films initiate the youth into the world of crime and make the vagabonds. However, the Children's Film Society India (CFSI) provides value based entertainment to children through the medium of films and is engaged in production, acquisition, distribution/exhibition and promotion of children's films. CFSI films are telecast regularly on Doordarshan as well as on private satellite channels.

Thus while cinema has many advantages, it also has a number of disadvantages. Our Government should, therefore, formulate a National Policy on Films so that only good and purposeful films are produced and exhibited in our country. The Censor Board should be told to be stricter while passing the films. If the right types of films with social and moral messages are produced, they can bring about the much needed reforms and changes in our society.

Role of Newspaper in India

An efficient and fearless press is one of the pre-requisites of a democracy. It would be apt if we call the press a mirror of society. It acts as a watch-dog of democracy where ideas and majority opinions prevail. It is the duty of the press to watch the activities of the Government, highlight its failure when it deviates from the path of democratic pattern and thereby force it to make up for its lapses.

In Indian democracy, most of the people are impoverished, illiterate and inarticulate; hence the newspapers have a special responsibility to take over the role of spokesman for people of all classes, to act as a bridge between the government and the governed, to prevent social exploitation that can threaten the existence of democracy.

The first newspaper was published in India in the mid-18th century by James A. Hicky. It was called *Bengal Gazette*. The oldest daily newspaper, the Bombay Samachar is being published in Gujarat since 1822. *Ananda Bazar Patrika*, *Punjab Kesari* and *Times of India* are the other old newspapers. Today the Indian Press has 41 centenarians.

The Office of the Registrar of Newspapers for India (RNI) came into existence on 1 July 1956, on the recommendation of the First Press Commission in 1953 and by amending the Press and Registration of Books Act, 1867. The Registrar of

Newspapers for India, commonly known as the Press Registrar, is required to submit an Annual Report to the Government by 31 December every year on the status of newspaper.

The period for which the annual statements were to be furnished, was changed from the calendar to financial year in 2002. Earlier the Annual Report was compiled on financial year basis. The total number of registered Newspapers/Periodical was 69,323 as on 31 March 2008. These were 7,710 dailies, 379 tri/bi-weeklies, 23,414 weeklies, 9,053 fortnightlies, 20,948 monthlies, 4,687 quarterlies, 605 annuals, and 2,518 of the other periodicity. (The figures have been updated only for the registered newspapers for the year 2007-08).

According to the report submitted by the Press Registrar for the year 2007-08, Newspapers were registered in 123 languages and dialects. Apart from English and 22 other principal languages listed in the Eighth Schedule of the Constitution, newspapers were registered in 100 other languages and dialects mostly Indian but also in a few foreign languages too. Orissa had the distinction of publishing newspapers in 18 out of 23 principle languages Maharashtra came next with publication in 17 languages followed by Delhi with publications in 16 principle languages.

Of the 69,323 newspapers registered as on 31 March 2008, only 9,072 submitted Annual Statements during 2007-08. The total circulation of these 9,072 newspapers was 20, 71,08,115 copies per publicity day. The largest number of newspapers and periodicals registered in any Indian language is in Hindi (25,527). The second largest number of newspapers and periodicals registered in any language is in English (10,000). The state with the largest number of registered newspaper is

Uttar Pradesh (10,799). The state with the second largest number of registered newspapers is Delhi (8,545).

The 2009 Indian Readership Survey findings show that the largest read local language newspapers to be Dainik Jagran (with 55.7 million readers) and Dainik Bhaskar (with 31.9 million readers), both published in Hindi. The Times of India is the most widely read English language newspaper (13.3 million), followed by Hindustan Times (6.3 million), The Hindu (5.2 million). The New Indian Express is another widely-read English language newspaper (1.8 million). Malayala Manorama newspaper which is published in Malayalam crossing 1.8 million has the largest circulation in regional languages.

The most significant nationalist newspaper was *Kesari*, founded by BAL Gangadhar Tilak in Bombay in January 1888. He emphasized that the traditional role of press was to be vigilant about public affairs. From the early part of the 20th century till 1947, the most decisive driving force behind all change in India and also its press was Mahatma Gandhi. So press played a dominant role during the pre-independence era.

In the post-Independence era also, the role of the press was up to the expectation. After India's defeat by China in 1962, Nehru's policy of friendship with China was fully exposed. When Mrs. Indira Gandhi censored the press during the Emergency she lost the elections due to lack of touch or awareness about the public mood. In modern days also, the press is playing an important role in educating people about the various issues which are directly or indirectly related with the life of Indian people.

In a democracy, newspapers are crucial both for the Government and the people. Newspapers inform the people of the programmes, policies and activities of the government. Similarly, they keep the government informed of the reactio1l of the people, their problems, grievances, hopes and aspirations. Newspapers thus serve as a bridge between the Government and the people. However, country ruled by a dictator, newspapers have to project the views. They do not enjoy freedom of expression. They cannot offer even constructive criticism.

Information is fed to the newspapers by a number of agencies. The Press Information Bureau is the central agency of the Government to give information to the Press on Government policies, programmes and activities, receive feedback from the people and advise the Government on its information policy. Besides, India has four news agencies–Press Trust of India (PTI). United News of India (UN I), Samachar Bharti and Hindustan Samachar. Non-Aligned countries have also set up a News Agencies pool. It is being operated by PTI.

In the past, the press in India played a great role by supporting the freedom movement launched by Mahatma Gandhi against the British rulers. Of course, the British always adopted a double standard while dealing with the English Press and the Vernacular Press. They tried their level best to gag the national press in India. Some of the editors of the newspapers were even jailed. Their only fault was that they criticised the British Government for its anti-India policy.

Newspaper circulations worldwide rose 2.3% in 2006 with Indian sales increasing most with 12.93%, the World Association of Newspapers (WAN) said on 4-06-07 Newspaper sales increased in Asia, Europe, Africa and South America, with North America the only continent to register a decline. Advertising revenues in paid dailies were up 3.77% in

2006, WAN said. China, Japan and India account for 60% of the world's 100 best-selling dailies, while the five largest markets for newspapers are China, India. Japan, the US and Germany. The circulation of Indian dailies jumped 33% to over 7.86 crore during 2001-2005 even as global newspaper circulation increased 9.95% in the same period. Contrary to conventional wisdom, newspaper circulation is growing and new newspapers are being launched at a remarkable rate, the Paris-based World Association of Newspapers (WAN) said in a release on 6-02-2007. Daily newspaper titles surpassed 10,000 for the first time in history, with India accounting for 1,834 dailies in 2005, up 22.8% from 1,493 dailies in 2001, according to World Press Trends.

The newspapers in India have a great future. They can help in the development of our country. They can highlight the social, economic and moral evils prevailing in our society and suggest ways and means to eradicate these evils. The main social evils are untouchability, dowry, drinking, child marriage, etc. They can also mobilize public opinion against economic evils like smuggling, black-marketing, tax evasion, hoarding, ticketless travelling, etc. They can also expose and fight corruption. In this manner, newspapers can render great service to India and its people.

Generation Gap

The gap between old people and young boys and girls is called the generation gap. While the young people are inexperienced, rash and impatient the elders are endowed with wisdom, prudence and caution. This gap between the two generations is not a new phenomenon. It has existed since time immemorial.

The people belonging to the older generation always wonder as to what has gone wrong with the new generation. They feel that during their time, young boys and girls were better behaved, more obedient, and had greater respect for their elders. They feel that a lack of respect for the old will bring ruin and spell disaster for the young. Young people, on the other hand, feel that they are capable enough to learn on their own rather than lean heavily on the older generation for any guidance. Young people do not like to be spoon-fed by their elders.

The gap between the old and the new generations is widening day-by-day due to various reasons. First of all, the young people feel that the present system of education has little relevance to the realities of life. It is not job–oriented. The result is that even after completing their schooling, they are not able to find any employment. They feel highly disillusioned.

Secondly, life has become so busy and fast that parents find little time to devote to their children. Efforts to promote intimacy and understanding between the old and the young are lacking.

Thirdly, the young also find that there is a difference between what they are expected to do and what is actually happening in the country. The talk of duty, dedication, morality, etc. leaves the young in a quandary. Young people are not prepared to follow whatever their elders tell them. When the young people find that corruption has entered into every sphere of life, they feel disgusted. They fight against social and economic injustice. They demand a change.

In India, tradition is still dominant. Tradition kills the initiative of younger generation. In order to express their disenchantment with the existing state of affairs, young people often resort to violence. They wear what they like. They behave in a very unconventional manner. They have no respect tradition, custom, manners etc. They develop an aversion to hard work.

The generation gap has widened to such an extent that the old and the young people appear to be living in two separate worlds without any interaction. In order to bridge this generation gap, elders should adopt a more sympathetic approach towards the young, and try to understand the emotions, the aspirations and the problems of the young. The youth should realize that they have no experience of life. They should, therefore, value the advice and counsel of the elders. If the youth have any difference of opinion, they should put across their viewpoint before the elders in a very polite and respectful manner.

In the western countries of Europe and America, the generation gap is so much that the young and the old do not like to live together. The young people start living separately as soon as they are able to earn their livelihood. Similarly, the old people also start living separately in their own houses or in Pensioner Houses or old age Homes in their old age. Thus this generation gap results in the break-up of homes and joint families.

Although under the influence of the western education the problem of generation gap is also creating a lot of problems in India, yet its effect is still limited in our country due to the influence of the joint family system prevailing in India. There are definitely a lot of advantages in the joint family system. Therefore, we should not follow the western system blindly at the cost of the well-tried Indian social and family tradition.

But this does not mean that the youth are always at fault. The real meaning of 'Generation Gap' is the lack of understanding between old and new generations. It should be the duty of both generations to try to understand and respect one another's views. Only then this problem can be solved.

India's Historical Monuments

It is said that India is dotted with monuments since antiquity. The country has a rich cultural heritage. Our ancient rulers had great fascination for magnificent buildings like forts, temples and mosques.

They built some of the most remarkable buildings in the world. Some of these buildings have vanished in the march of time but many like Taj Mahal, Lai Quila, Qutub Minar, Jama Masjid, Fatehpur Sikri, Caves of Ajanta and Ellora, Sarnath Temple have stood the test of time. The British have also played an important role in giving us some historical monuments.

Temple art flourished in the Gupta period architecture. Dashavtar Temple of Degaru is the first example of making Shekhar (top) in temple art. Brahma cave temples and Buddha cave temples are important among Gupta period caves temples.

The main temples of Gupta period are:

Bhimrao (Nagged) (Shiva)

Toga (Jabalpur) (Vishnu)

Degaru (Jhansi) (Dashavtar)

Syrup (brick made) (Layman)

Udayagiri (Vishnu)

Bitargaon (Kanpur, brick made) (Shiva)

Kho (Nagod) (Shiva)

The rock-cut architecture of the period is represented by two conventional types–the Chaitya and the Vihara. They are mostly found at Ajanta, Ellora and Bagh. The special feature of Chaitya is its emphasis on the colossal image of Buddha seated between two attendants. The Vihara was in the form of rows of cells around a central court. The most number of Viharas are to be found at Ajanta.

These caves are remarkable for the variety and beauty of the pillars and the fine fresco paintings with which the walls and ceilings are decorated. The Gupta period is the formative and creative age heralding the two important styles, Nagara and Dravida? Of the stupas built during this period, the one at Mirpur Khas in Sindh and Dhamesh at Sarnath is most remarkable. The Iron Pillar of Mehrauli, near Delhi, is another excellent monument of Gupta period.

The Chalukyan style of temple architecture equated with versara style is seen as an admixture of the Dravida and Nagara styles of temple architecture. Like the Dravida style, the Chalukya style of temples has two principal components, the vimana and the mandappa, joined by an antarala. Famous temples of this period include the Virupaksha temple at Pattdakal near Badami, the Vishnu temple of Badami, the Shiva temple of Maguti and the Kashi Visveswara temple of Lakhundi.

Krishna I built the famous rock-cut Kailash temple at Ellora in the latter half of the eighth century AD. It was built in the Dravidian style of the Chalukyas and elaborately carved with fine sculptures. The cave shrine of Elephanta was built in the second half of the eighth century, on an island near the west coast. It was dedicated to Shiva in his image as Mahesha.

The credit for having initiated the rock architecture in the

Pallava Dynasty must be given to the royal artist Mahendra Varman I. Some of his architectural works are the cave temples on the hill at Mandagappattu, the five-celled cave temple at Pallavaram near Chennai, the four cave temples at Mamandur and the Siva temple at Sivamargalam. A few Vishnu cave temples on the hill at Mamandur and the Siva temples at Sivamargalam a few Vishnu cave temples were also excavated by Mahendra Varman.

The Hoysalas were great temple builders, the finest examples of which are the Kesava temple at Belur (in Hassan district) and Halebid (Dwarasamudra).

The chief features of the Chola temples are vimanas or towers, which were later eclipsed by the richly ornamented gopurams or gateways. One of the finest examples of Cholas style is, however, provided by Brihadeshwara temple at Tanjore, built by Rajraja I. The temple of Gangaikonda-Cholapuram is another fine example of temple architecture under the Cholas.

The Chandellas built magnificent temples at Khajuraho. Chausath Yogni temple is most prominent among these temples.

Rajput rulers made many historical buildings. Amber Fort, Hawa Mahal, Fort of Chittor, etc. are historical monuments of India. Victory Tower at Chittor is also a remarkable monument built by Raja Kumbha.

The new features of architecture brought by the Turkish conquerors were *(i)* the dome, *(ii)* lofty towers, *(iii)* the vault, and *(iv)* the true arch unsupported by beam.

The most magnificent building constructed by Turks in the 13th century was Qutub Minar. This tapering tower, originally 71.4 metres high and built by Iltutmish, was dedicated to the

Sufi saint Qutub-ub-din Bakhtiyar Kaki, who was greatly respected by all the people of Delhi.

Quwwatul-Islam Mosque, built by Qutub-ud-din, in Delhi is another remarkable example of the architecture of the Ilbari Turk Dynasty. The Arhai-Din Ka Jhonpra at Ajmer started by Qutub-ud-din Aibek has an exquisitely carved mehrab of white marble and a decorative arch screen and a beautiful prayer hall. The premier example of true arch is said to be the tomb of Ghyas-ud-din Balban in Mehrauli. Balban made Lal Mahal in Delhi.

Ala-ud-din Khilji added an entrance door to the Qutub. This door, which is called the Alai Darwaza, has arches of very pleasing propositions. It also contains a doer which, for the first time, was built on correct scientific lines.

The Tughaq buildings show stark simplicity and sobriety- probably indicating less financial resources as well as a puritanical taste. The buildings are characterised by sloping walls and a dark appearance. Tughlaq monuments are the fort at Tughlaqabad, the tomb of Ghyas-ud-din Tughlaq which marked a new phase in Indo-Islamic architecture by serving as a model for later tombs, the fort of Adilabad, Firuz Shah's capital at Delhi, now known as Kotla Firuz Shahi and a group of buildings at Hauz Khas in Delhi with Firuz Shah's Tomb.

Moth ki Masjid erected by the Prime Minister or Sikandar Lodhi is a magnificent monument of medieval period. The building shows elegance with the use of enamelled tiles–a technique introduced from Persia.

Husan Shah erected Jami Masjid, his dome and Hindola Mahal. Jahaj Mahal was erected by Sultan Mahmood I. These are classical monuments of Islamic architecture.

Imbrahim Sharki erected Atala Masjid and Jhanjori Masjid. Hussain Shah Sharki constructed Jami Masjid and Lal Darwaja.

Ahmed Shah I erected Jami Masjid in Ahmedabad. It is an excellent monument of Gujarat style. The famous Nagina Masjid was built by Mahmood Baigra.

Chhoti Sona Masjid, Bari Sona Masjid, and Lotan Masjid are famous monuments in Gaud. Adina Masjid in Pandua, built by Sikander Shah is another magnificent monument.

The famous Hazara Rama Swami Temple built during Krishnadeva Raya's reign is described as "a perfect specimen of Hindu temple and architecture". Fergusson, the great art critic, has described the famous Yithal Temple as the "true replica of Dravidian style-a distinct school of architecture".

Several excellent monuments were built during the Mughal Period.

Sher Shah, who dispossessed Humayun, was a great builder. The most remarkable monuments of his time are the mosque in the Purana Quila Delhi and his own tomb at Sasaram in Bihar. Akbar mostly used red stone in his buildings. One of his earliest buildings was the tomb of Humayun at Delhi.

He built magnificient buildings in Agra such as the fort, the Diwan-i- Aam, the Diwan-i-Khas and the palace known as Jahangiri Mahal. The most impressive monuments are the tomb of Salim Chisti, the Panch Mahal, Buland Darwaza and Jodha Bai Palace at Fatehpur Sikri constructed by Akbar. Akbar combined Persian, Indian and Central Asian styles. His mausoleum at Sikandara is a unique building modelled on the Buddhist Viharas of India. It was planned by Akbar, but built by Jahangir.

Jahangir also made the tomb of Itimad-ud-daulah. It was built in white marble and is one of the earliest buildings to be decorated with pietra dura or inlaying of semi-precious stones of different colours. In fact, it was built by Nur Jahan over the grave of her father.

Shah Jehan was a most prolific and magnificient builder. Taj Mahal is a world renowned excellent monument erected by Shah Jahan over the grave of his beloved wife Mumtaz Mahal. Pietra dura work, delicate marble screens and chhatris are special artistic features in this monument. It took twenty-two years (1631-53) to build and cost about three crores of rupees. Twenty thousand workmen were employed to construct it.

Diwan-i-Aam, Diwan-i-Khas at Red Fort, Jama Masjid in Delhi, and Moti Masjid in Agra are remarkable monuments built by Shah Jehan.

The Pear Mosque or the Moti Masjid was also built at Agra inside the fort at a cost of Rs. 300,000. It is one of the most beautiful buildings made of white marble.

Mussamman Burj is a beautiful octagonal structure of marble in the fort of Agra. Shah Jehan died here. From this place the Emperor could see the Taj.

Lal Qila or the Red Fort stands in Delhi on the right bank of the Yamuna. It contains the Diwan-i-Aam (Hall of Public Audience) and the Diwan-i-Khas (Hall of Private Audience). The latter has a marble water channel running through it, which enhances its beauty.

Jama-i-Masjid is another remarkable historical monument which stands at some distance opposite the Red Fort in Delhi. It is one of the finest and biggest mosques in the world and can accommodate thousands of people. It is made of red sandstone and white marble.

Victoria Memorial and Writers' Buildings in Kolkata and India Gate in New Delhi are the notable historical monuments of the modern period erected by the British during their 200-year rule in this country. Some people even blame them for tempering with some parts of architecture of Taj Mahal. They uprooted one of the fountains to see how it worked, but were not able to fix it back.

India has a number of remarkable monuments in almost every part of the country, but it is a matter of shame that almost all of them are in a state of neglect. The governments at the centre and the concerned state are trying their best to keep their sanctity and beauty, but unless people realize the importance of preserving these symbols of India's heritage, these monuments will continue to suffer.

Global Warming

Global warming is the greatest challenge facing our planet. It is, in fact, the increase in the temperature of the earth's neon-surface air. It is one of the most current and widely discussed factors. It has far-reaching impact on biodiversity and climatic conditions of the planet. Several current trends clearly demonstrate that global warming is directly impacting on rising sea levels, the melting of ice caps and significant worldwide climate changes. In short, global warming represents a fundamental threat to all living things on earth.

Global average temperature rose significantly during the past century. The prevailing scientific view is that most of the temperature increases since mid-20th century has been caused by increases in atmospheric greenhouse gas concentrations produced by human activity. Most scientists agree that planet's temperature has risen 0.5 degree Celsius since 1900 and will continue to increase at an increasing rate. As a result, the world is getting warmer. The year 1990 was the hottest year in the last century.

Together with 1991, the years of 1983, 1987, 1988 and 1989 have been measured to be the warmest six years in the last hundred years. The year 1991 was the second warmest year of the past century. The consequences of the rise in temperature is being felt all over the globe the findings of scientific research done in this field reveal that the temperature of the earth is likely to rise from 1.4°C to 5.8°C within a period of 100 years.

Unfortunately, the imbalance which we have created between our life and earth is already showing the signs disasters in the form of flood, cyclones, landslides, tsunami, drought, etc. If the imbalance continues to rise, one day this will pose a question mark on the existence of this planet. Carbon dioxide (CO2) which is an important constituent of environment is causing a warming effect on the earth's surface.

It increases the evaporation of water into the atmosphere. Since water vapour itself is a greenhouse gas, this causes still more warming. The warming causes more water vapour to be evaporated. The CO2 level is expected to rise in future due to ongoing burning of fossil fuels and landuse change. The rate of rise will depend largely on uncertain economic, sociological, technological and natural developments. Other gases such as methane, CFCs, nitrous oxide, tropospheric ozone are also responsible for global warming. Increases in all these gases are due to explosive population growth, increased industrial expansion, technological advancement, deforestation and growing urbanisation, etc.

Trees play a significant role in the global carbon cycle. They are the largest land-based mechanism for removing carbon dioxide from the air. Deforestation is checking these positive processes. It is the second principle cause of atmospheric carbon dioxide. Deforestation is responsible for 25 per cent of all carbon emissions entering the atmosphere, by the burning and cutting of 34 million acres of trees each year. Everyday over 5500 acres of rainforest are destroyed. As a consequence of massive loss of forests, global CO2, levels rise approximately 0.4 per cent each year, the levels not experienced on this planet for millions of years. As we know the forests are the great absorbers of CO2,.

There is a close relation between global warming and population growth. Today the large population on earth is using the technologies which are destructive for the earth. Approximately, 80 per cent of atmospheric CO2 increases are due to man's use of fossil fuels either in the form of coal, gas or oil. A large portion of carbon emission is attributed to the burning of gasoline in internal-combustion engine of vehicles. Vehicles with poor gas mileage contribute the most to global warming. Besides, the sulphur group gas is the most harmful for this. Its contribution is 30 per cent in global warming. This gas is also emitted from the burning of fossil fuels.

Increase in global temperatures will cause rise in sea level. It will lead to melting of glaciers, changes in rainfall patterns, increased intensity and frequency of extreme weather. As per the latest survey report the rate of melting of glaciers has seen sharp increase in recent times. Even those glaciers are affected from global warming which have been considered permanent. The shrinking of glaciers is going to pose a major problem of drinking water.

The sea levels as a result of melting of glaciers have risen from 0.35 mm to 0.4 mm. Scientists have warned in their reports that most of the glaciers will disappear within a period of 15 to 25 years. It will create problems of drinking water and food grains in most of the North American countries. India is not unaffected from it. The Himalayan glaciers have shrunk about 30 per cent after 1970.

The rise in sea levels is a major cause of concern. A large number of cities located in coastal areas will submerge in the sea. Besides, many island countries will ultimately "lose their existence and will be washed away from the surface of the earth. The damage of rising sea levels is diverse. Buildings and roads close to the water could be flooded and they could suffer damage from hurricanes and tropical storms. Experts believe that global warming could increase the intensity of hurricanes by over 50 per cent. In addition, as the sea rises, beach erosion takes place, particularly on steep banks.

Wetlands are lost as the level rises. Rise in atmospheric temperature will lead to the outbreak of air-borne and water-borne diseases. It would also contribute to the rise in death caused by heat. The problem of drought would be frequent. Consequently, malnutrition and starvation will pose serious challenge before humanity.

Global warming is a great threat to the flora and fauna of the earth. A large number of species of them may become extinct.

The expanse of desert would increase. Low rainfall and rising temperature could add to the intensity and frequency of dusty storm. This in turn will immensely affect the quality of agricultural land, ultimately causing adverse effect on agricultural produce. It would have far-reaching socio-economic impact.

In Indian context, the impact of global warming is a matter of grave concern. As is well known, India is mainly an agricultural country and agriculture here is gamble of the monsoon, e.g. largely depending on rainfall. Though it is to affect the whole country, the worst likely impact would be on central and northern India which is high-yielding parts of the country. These are the regions which produce the largest agricultural yield. The rise in atmospheric temperature and fall in rain would naturally result in decline in crop production. Moreover, it would have great effect on biodiversity as well.

The growing concerns over global temperatures have led to the nations, states, corporations and individuals to draw out a plan of action to avert the situation. As a result the world's primary international agreement on combating global warming was reached in Kyoto in 1997 which came to be known as Kyoto Protocol. However, ten years have passed; the situation does not appear to be very changed. It seems that the member countries are not very serious about its devastating effects.

In addition, forestation can be of great help in this regard. Planting more trees and reducing timber cuts worldwide will help restore the imbalance. Secondly, we must follow on environmental policy of 'reduce, reuse, recycle', i.e. promoting the reuse of anything. Thirdly, the use of fuel-efficient vehicles should be promoted as these vehicles have lower emissions of harmful gases. Fourthly, every individual should be aware of the importance of the protecting environment. Besides, eco-friendly technologies must be promoted, and must be substituted with the technologies which cause great emission of global warming gases. Public awareness campaign can be of great help in this regard because unless each and every individual is aware only governments' effect cannot bring desired difference.

Benefits of Exercise

We exercise all the time without even thinking of it. Just being active, like when we run around outside or play kickball at school, is a kind of exercise. What else counts as exercise? Playing sports, dancing, doing push-ups and even reaching down to touch our toes.

When we exercise, we are helping build a strong body that will be able to move around and do all the stuff we need it to do. Try to be active every day and our body will thank we later!

We may know that our heart is a muscle. It works hard, pumping blood every day of our life. We can help this important muscle get stronger by doing aerobic exercise.

Aerobic means 'with air', so aerobic exercise is a kind of activity that requires oxygen. When we breathe, we take in oxygen and, if we ere doing aerobic exercise, we may notice we are breathing faster than normal. Aerobic activity can get our heart pumping, make we sweaty and quicken our breathing.

When we give our heart this kind of workout on a regular basis, our heart will get even better at its main job-delivering oxygen (in the form of oxygen-carrying blood cells) to all parts of our body

Swimming, basketball, ice or roller hockey, jogging (or walking quickly), in-line skating, soccer, cross-country skiing, biking or rowing are some of the examples of aerobic exercises. And don't forget that skipping, jumping rope and playing hopscotch are aerobic activities, too!

Another kind of exercise can help make our muscles stronger. We do a push-up or swing across the monkey bars at the playground? Those are exercises that can build strength. By using our muscles to do powerful things, we can make them stronger. For older teens and adults, this kind of workout can make muscles bigger, too.

Here are some exercises and activities to build strong muscles:

- push-ups
- pull-ups
- tug-of-war
- rowing
- running
- in-line skating
- bike riding

Many children are flexible, which means that they can bend and stretch their bodies without much trouble. This kind of exercise often feels really good, like when we take a big stretch in the morning after waking up. Being flexible is having 'full range of motion', which means we can move our arms and legs freely without feeling tightness or pain. It's easy to find things to do for good flexibility:

- tumbling and gymnastics
- yoga
- dancing, especially ballet
- martial arts
- simple stretches, such as touching our toes or side stretches

Food gives our body fuel in the form of calories, which are

a kind of energy. Our body needs a certain amount of calories every day just to function, breathe, walk around and do all the basic stuff.

But if we are active, our body needs an extra measure of calories or energy. If we are not very active, our body won't need as many calories. Whatever our calorie need is, if we eat enough to meet that need, our body weight will stay about the same. If we eat more calories than our body needs, it may be stored as excess fat.

It feels good to have a strong, flexible body that can do all the activities we enjoy — like running, jumping and playing with our friends. It is also fun to be good at something, like scoring a basket, hitting a home run or perfecting a dive. But we may not know that exercising can actually put us in a better mood.

When we exercise, our brain releases a chemical called endorphins, which may make us feel happier. It's just another reason why exercise is cool!

Alcohol and its Effect

Alcohol is a central nervous system depressant– it slows down the body's functions and its effects are similar to those of a general anesthetic. Ethyl alcohol (ethanol) is the active ingredient in all alcoholic drinks.

If you take any alcoholic beverage and remove the ingredients that give it taste and colour, you get ethyl alcohol. Remove the water from ethyl alcohol and you get ether.

Ether is an anesthetic that works on the brain and puts it to sleep. The same symptoms surgical patient experiences under ether are those experienced by a person drinking alcohol.

Alcoholism

Alcohol consumption is a learned behaviour– no one likes the taste of alcohol at first. People drink out of curiosity, because of custom (let's "toast" the bride and groom), or escape from an unpleasant feeling with a sense of well-being and euphoria. Alcoholics are perceived as being weak people or as having bad habits.

Alcoholism is the disease produced by the repeated misuse of ethyl alcohol. It is a Primary disease: it is not caused by some underlying psychological or moral flaw. It is a chronic disease: it does not go away with time. It is a Progressive disease: it does not improve as long as one continues to drink. It is a potentially Fatal disease, if the drinking is not interrupted.

A primary characteristic of an alcoholic is a loss of control- once an alcoholic starts to drink, he or she is not able to predict things or situations in a normal way.

Alcohol and the Body

Once alcohol is absorbed into the bloodstream, it is rapidly distributed throughout the body. It affects almost every cell, every organ, and every level of human functioning, .The most profound early effect is on the central nervous system, where it acts as a sedative, producing relaxation and sense of well-being. It impairs the intellect, physical abilities and metabolism.

When alcohol is taken regularly, in large amounts over many years, permanent physical damage will occur. This damage is often aggravated by the lack of vitamins because most alcoholics have poor eating habits. Alcohol can also damage the liver, brain and other parts of the nervous system. In the final stages of alcoholism, parts of the brain are permanently damaged and confusion, disorientation and DT's result.

Alcohol and the Brain

Any chemical that alters mood, feelings, co-ordination, perception, or behaviour, alters the cells in the brain and disrupts their normal chemical behaviour.

When alcohol enters the blood stream it travels to the brain. Alcohol can affect millions of nerve cells and change communication patterns throughout the brain. Alcohol can impair vision, distort hearing, muddle speech, impair judgement, dull the body's senses, disturb motor skills, and reduce co-ordination. Deep inside the brain alcohol can affect the areas that control aggression, hunger and thirst, pleasure and pain, and body temperature.

These effects are produced because alcohol inhibits blood from transporting oxygen to brain cells. When brain cells are deprived of oxygen, they become impaired and possibly die! That's brain damage.

Because the brain matures more slowly than other organs of the body, it may be even more susceptible to certain permanent, irreversible effects of alcohol.

The hypothalamus is the portion of the brain that controls our automatic reflexes: breathing, heartbeat, and other bodily operations over which an individual has no conscious control. When alcohol is present in the blood stream it directly affects the hypothalamus, possibly damaging it, particularly during the adolescent years.

In addition, alcohol has a profound effect on the frontal lobe– the part of the brain that allows us to analyse and programme our behaviour. It also allows us to convert experience to memory and is responsible for the formation of our "self-image". These processes require a tremendous amount of energy. The depressant nature of alcohol directly lowers die energy centre in the brain. Those who lower the energy levels in the brain by using alcohol or other toxic chemicals, lose not only mental capacity, but their ability to realise they have lost it.

Alcohol and the Unborn Child

Alcohol is carried from your blood through the placenta and enters your baby's blood, circulating through your foetus. Your baby is then dependent on your excretory system to remove the alcohol. Exposure to alcohol can represent a serious risk to your child. Women who drink during their pregnancies double the risk of having a baby born with physical or mental handicaps.

Foetal Alcohol Effects refer to birth defects as a result of alcohol use during pregnancy. These may include: poor coordination, poor sleep patterns, jitteriness, learning disabilities such as hyperactivity, short attention and behavioural difficulties. Most of these are problems that will last a lifetime.

Foetal Alcohol Syndrome is one of most serious conditions associated with drinking during pregnancy. It is characterized by low birth weight, small head, mental retardation and failure to thrive and grow properly. A recent study has found that a father's drinking habits during the month of his child's conception can affect his baby's birth weight.

Books: A Treasure House of Knowledge

Books are wonderful gifts to mankind. Books are useful in many ways. They educate, entertain and serve as good companions when we are lonely. They guide us when we are confused. They inspire us when we are low in spirit. They are men's best friends. Books console us when we are in sorrow. We are never alone in the company of books. They demand nothing for the service they do to the mankind.

The kingdom of books is as vast as universe. There are books on literature, science, fiction, history, art, culture, civilisation, architecture, fashion, technology, philosophy, etc. Some books are for serious reading, some are intended to enrich our knowledge and learning. Many books give us an insight into various aspect of life. Books on travel and adventure infuse into us a spirit of fearlessness and adventure. The reading of novels is a pleasant pastime for many of us. This provides an escape from the din and bustle of life. One is completely lost in the company of good books. There is no sphere of life which has not been explored by the books.

Books are good source of dissemination of useful ideas. They are effective tools to popularize the fruits of our research in various fields of knowledge. They help in the spread of our progressive views. They are reservoir of knowledge and information. They pass the knowledge and information from generation and generation. In fact, no single labour of human fruit has been as helpful to the advancement of civilization as books. Books are written in all languages of the world.

The advancement of science and technology has brought about a great change in the field of books. Five centuries back, the books as we have today did not exist. But machines and technology have helped in the spread of knowledge. Moreover, the high percentage of literacy, the growth of libraries in towns and villages and growing fondness of the intellectuals to have their private libraries have led to the growth of publishing industry. This in turn contributed to the spread of knowledge and information. Books are written by experienced persons who are wise and have matured minds. They are full of ideas, and thoughts which enlighten us and guide us at the time of trouble. There are books which entertain, enthrall and thrill us according to our taste.

Different people have different tastes and choices. As one grows old, one's interest and taste also changes. A child may be crazy for comics, picture, story books or works of science fiction. Some people have great love for books. Books are their permanent friends. They carry them wherever they go.

Books help to widen our interest. They broaden our outlook. They enrich our thoughts. They help us in understanding different aspects of life. They give us inspiration to do great things in life. They encourage us to fight the odds of life bravely. They fill our minds with noble thoughts. They awaken our souls. They mould our characters. But we should be very cautious in the choice of books. Books which are not good may mislead the readers. They can spoil us.

Thus, books are a blessing. They are the treasure richer than the treasure of the king. This treasure is inexhaustible. They are the gold mines of art, literature, science and information. We should develop a habit of reading. It is good for us and society as well.

Computer Addiction

There once was a time when the only computers known to the average person were those the military possessed. Eventually, large corporations found many different uses for computers in the business world, and today, computers are as common in numerous households around the globe. People from all age groups are learning to operate computers and anyone who has worked with computers for long periods of time knows that computers can be just as addicting as smoking. Computer addiction can have a number of physical, social, and psychological effects on a person and it is to be taken as seriously as any other addiction that a person is battling. One common physical effect computer addiction can have on a person are back problems. Sitting for so long can take a toll on a person's muscles and can result in poor posture. Poor posture can result in chronic back problems that require the services of a chiropractor. Dry eyes, carpal tunnel syndrome, and vision complications are some eye problems caused by over use of a computer. Migraine headaches are quite common in computer addiction and are linked to the straining of the eyes. Because of the long hours spent engrossed in a computer, addicts often have eating irregularities, such as skipping meals and binge eating.

Computer addicts experience sleep disturbances, or changes in sleeping patterns, which are most likely due to late hours on the computer and low blood sugar from eating irregularities. One last effect is the failure to attend to personal hygiene, such as bathing, combing hair and brushing teeth. All of these physical effects can be linked to computer addiction. Social effects of computer addiction include reduced time spent socializing with others. People may begin to feel that their computer is the only relationship that they have the time to focus on. They lose the desire for human contact and communication and in a way they are breaking away from reality. Lacking the desire to make contact with others, means lacking the desire to create new relationships or to build on already existing ones. After a certain amount of time, they lose their conversation skills completely. Within the lives of computer addicts it is their friends and family that suffer the most from this form of alienation. They are often moved to the very bottom of the computer addict's list of priorities.

Computer addiction has the power to cause serious social effects and cannot be left untreated. Along with the physical and social effects of computer addiction there are also psychological effects. Some psychological symptoms experienced by computer addicts when they are not at the computer are feelings of depression, emptiness, irritability, distraction and withdrawal. Feelings that are common when addicts are at the computer are a sense of euphoria or well-being. These senses of complete ecstasy and pleasure also causes and inability for people who are addicted to computers to stop the activity. They end up having a constant craving for more time at the computer, and this is where one can identify an addiction. Along with addiction comes a need to cover up their secret and computer addicts often lie to those around them. For example lying to employers, and family members about their hours spent at the computer and also denying they have a problem. This lying a sneaking around eventually results in problems either at school or at work. The psychological effects of computer addiction may not only lead to distraction and emptiness but may also lead to critical depression. When people think of addictions, no one ever thinks of computer addiction to actually be common. In this age of computers, computer addiction will only increase as time passes. More and more people will experience the physical, social, and psychological effects of computer addiction but, thankfully, like other addictions, this condition is treatable.

Scientific Temper and Rational Planning

"Realizing these limitations of reason and scientific method, we have still to hold on to them with all our strength, for without that firm basis and background we can, have no grip on any kind of truth or reality".

These are a large number of people in our society who have formally studied or are studying science, clearly driven by job expectations. This has caused the retreat of traditional values and a degree of modernization and homogenization of society, it is now certainly far less segregated along lines of caste, language or religion. Those who are engaged in industry, business and' commerce have no time to determine what identity their counterparts belong to. This is certainly a major achievement in free India.

However, if one looks at some of our fundamental problems, there is much cause for dismay and disappointment. Take the question of population. Even 50 years ago. At the time of Independence, the Indian subcontinent was already crowded. Today's India is adding in population in terms an Australia every year. But we are not adding to our resource base in the same proportion.

Irrationality is the lack of access to safe drinking water and sanitary toilets for a large majority of our population, while a small segment is busy with star TV, CNN, MTV and so on.

After independence a substantial and comprehensive base of science and technology has been created and several scientists and technologists trained. Among the laboratories of the Council of Scientific and Industrial Research, there have been some very good examples of integration with application. To mention only two : the Central Leather Research Institute has done well to help export leather goods; the National Chemical Laboratory too has a good record of working with industry.

The other laboratories, in spite of high quality manpower and facilities, have not yet been able to upgrade industry or provide new designs and processes. A recent move to make them earn fifty per cent of their operating cost outside of the government funds, may force them to integrate with industry.

Agriculture has seen a really successful tieup between the laboratories and the farms. We must continue their association as agriculture will now face another revolution based on biotechnological innovations, it is in atomic energy and space sciences, where the applications have been tightly knit with laboratory work, that progress has been really very impressive. Indian scientists and technologist expected that links between the laboratories and application areas would be strengthened, and that we would soon see a strong, self reliant industrial and agricultural development.

But now we face irrationality. The opening up of the economy and liberalization, after four decades of regulation and control, has been widely welcomed. If the new open door policy succeeds, India Is expected to have large manufacturing bases for products of multinationals, hopefully supplying an overseas market with goods that will compete globally in price, quality and performance. This could happen at least in a range of products where our resource base would augment the advantage of lowcost skilled labour.

On the other hand, we will only be manufacturing to designs evolved in one of the advanced countries. The design capability we have built up is in danger of wilting. The exceptions would be where the MWCs find it' profitable to integrate Indian design effort into their mainline work. This is likely to be limited.

What are the prospects of product of Indian technology

breaking into the export market? Software export has been growing well and there is considerable scope for expansion. As a general rule, the scale of manufacture has been small. Even our larger activities would be mini or micro in international comparison. Many of these industries have been too small to support independent design effort, let alone research and development. There is a real danger to the survival of many of these industries In the face of competition from overseas giants who can indulge in price cutting and dumping with takeovers, dismantling of any line of manufacture could easily happen in the guise of rationalization.

Why is it important for India to continue its faith in selfreliance? Many people would point out that many economics such as those of South Korea, Taiwan, Thailand, Indonesia, Malaysia and others have done well in growing as part of international division of labour. Let us recall that Indian with a population of 800 million and China with over one billion are the two potentially largest economies. They will grow for the next several decades. They will therefore, be large markets for both capital goods and consumer articles.

India will continue to build power stations, extended electricity supplies, add to its fleet of trucks, modernise the railway system, build petroleum refineries, and so on. Equally, the consumer demands for automobiles, two wheelers, TV sets and so forth will also continue. It is important, therefore, that we not only manufacture these articles in the country but also improve them with newer designs based on research and development undertaken in the country. There is a need to integrate ourselves into the global economy at our own pace as equal partners but not be stamped into joining as second class citizen.

Whenever one defends the policy of the opening up of our economy the case is on the basis of bringing in the latest technology required to rapidly build up the nation. Quite often we end up getting technology, for soft drinks or fast food. Verghese Kurien posed the question "Why do we need to import the technology for potato chips?" A news item talks about the entry to India of the American fast food chain, Mc Donalds. The entry is justified on the ground that it would attract overseas tourists.

The list of irrationalities does not end here. At another level, there is the irrationality of the Indian Science Congress instituting an award for astrology. Another irrationality staring us in the face is the Dunkel Draft that is being negotiated by the GATT. Western Pharmaceutical companies have complained in the past about India's patent laws. Even if, these laws did not suit them, the country has been able to supply lifesaving drugs at affordable prices. Under the new dispensation, this may not be so.

Even more ominous are the provisions relating to intellectual property rights as they apply to agriculture. According to noted agricultural scientist M.S. Swaminathan, free flow of knowledge across national frontiers helped the growth of agriculture and animal husbandry worldwide. The provisions, of the Dunkel Draft favour Europe and North America and mitigate against the developing countries. Even in the field of computer software, the Dunkel provisions mitigate against the hours. In a number of cases, court orders were wrongly interpreted to the chagrin of the affected parties, forcing them to go the High Court or the Supreme Court for contempt proceedings.

Not surprisingly, the system of ready justice dispensed by

criminals and antisocial elements with the connivance of political parties is finding increasing acceptance in society. The Kini murder case is only the tip of the iceberg. Political parties are not prepared to take up the cudgels against the trend. Rather, they denigrate the judiciary.

It is not therefore, surprising that the leaders of political parties at the national level are talking of reasserting the supremacy of Parliament vis-a-vis the judiciary and of amending the Prevention of Corruption Act to exclude the elected representatives from its purview and so on. There is also a move to amend the provisions of the Constitution to bring the judiciary under the undisputed hold of the executive in the matter of appointment and transfers of judges of the higher judiciary. The latest in this series of the proposed onslaughts is the move to curtail the scope of Public Interest Litigation by making it obligatory for the applicant to pay a deposit of ₹ 1 lakh and to confine the eligibility of the applicants to those who are below the poverty line and so on.

The arrogance and insensitivity of the executive at the State and Central levels were decisively brought home recently once again by its actions of invoking the provisions of the Official Secrets Act. In a recent PIL case in the Bombay High Court pertaining to the reported death of over 1.000 children during the last four, years in the tribal area of Melghat in Amravati district, the Maharashtra Government took the unbelievable stand that the two reports of inquiry made by Secretaries to the Government could not be made available s they were secret. Fortunately, the court did not uphold this plea and directed that they be made available to the parties to the litigation immediately. The other PIL on an equally vital public issue—the safety standards in nuclear establishments—asked whether precautions were being taken conforming to international standards and whether the regulatory and overseeing institutional arrangements were adequate. Again, a plea of the matter being secret was taken in the court by the Government of India. Unfortunately, the court accepted the plea and dismissed the PIL.

As it happens, the State Government concerned is being ruled by a coalition of the Shiv Sena and the BJP, and the Centre by a coalition of 13 political parties with Congress support. Therefore, in a sense, almost all political parties are partners in making a mockery of an open, transparent and responsible government which a democracy is expected to provide. It also shows their disregard for the judicial process and judicial review in such areas of critical public interest.

This inevitably raises the question of the direction in which the Indian democracy is heading. Sooner than later, the question which Mr. Thackeray asked "Who rules this country, the executive or the judiciary," will have to be answered in no uncertain terms. It is the rule of law which governs the country. The executive or the judiciary or Parliament are mere instrumentalities. It is a travesty of truth to say that during the 50th anniversary of our Independence, answers to such basic questions are still unclear to the ruling political elite.

International Co-operation through Science and Technology

In the history of human cooperation science and technology have played a crucial role, though its more sensational contributions have often been in the realm of conflict and warfare. From the invention of gun powder to nuclear weapons and the mind boggling programme of Star Wars, it was in the military sphere that international impact of science and technology has been felt environment, ozone depletion and global warming. Notwithstanding such precedents of our officers dealing with almost any subject under the sun, it is essential for the success of the economic-cum-technological diplomacy of the present-day world that there is direct association of scientists in bilateral and international negotiations and also regular and structure inter-action between scientists and diplomats. Some general training in some of the major areas of science and technology should also be considered an indispensable qualifications for modern diplomats.

It is only tension among nations, scramble for markets, territorial disputes, pursuit of power, accumulation of nuclear weapons and race for armaments, which today pose threats to peace and to the future of mankind, but unrestrained growth of population, menace of drugs and AIDS, destruction of the environment, the greenhouse effect, ozone depletion and global warming. All these require cooperative action at the international level involving politics, economics, social engineering, and all the resources of science and technology. It is believed that science and technology can play a crucial role in finding solutions to these global problems. But it can provide only part of the answer, not the whole answer. Indeed one has to go a little beyond politics, economics and science to find answers to the overwhelming questions facing mankind today.

When we talk of science and technology for resolving problems and bettering the condition of mankind, we often mean mainly producing and providing more and more of the good glittering things of life. We need more and more things, firstly, for satisfying the unfulfilled basic needs of millions of under-privileged and for meeting the needs of a rapidly growing population, and secondly, for catering to the craves of the well-to-do for endlessly multiplying wants and luxuries. For these purposes, perhaps more for the latter then for the former, we use technology for producing more and more, and better and still better goods and gadgets. We explore and discover new resources, we split the atom and the genes, we score the depths of oceans and conquer space believing that the hunger of man for lucre and power could be satisfied in this manner.

Intoxicated by the material possibilities held out by science, we do not ask whether some limitation upon the wants and cravings of man are not as much necessary, at least after a certain level of satisfaction, as producing an abundance of goods and services. We do not ask if the advancement of science should not be accompanied by the improvement of man including a civilized sense of self-restraint. It seems that even the fullest utilization of science and technology will not be able to satisfy the unlimited wants and desires of man and his greed for power and the symbols of power.

To some of the social and environmental problems created by technology; part of the answer is further development of technology itself like devices for controlling pollution including CFC emissions, developing alternatives to these so called "gases of prosperity" and technologies for conservation of energy, alternative sources of energy, etc. In all this intensified international cooperation is essential, but on the basis of developmental equity for the countries of the South.

Thus, without being altruistic and sacrificing their legitimate economic interests it should be possible for the developed countries of the world to be guided by this spirit of sharing in the sphere of international cooperation in science and technology. That would, besides, be an indication that the development of the awesome power of science and technology will be animated by the spirit of humanism for the good of mankind and not for purposes of exploitation or destruction.

Forests—Need For Conservation

Trees are mankind's lifeline. If they are destroyed, there is no way that human beings can survive. From the oxygen that we breathe in, the food that we eat, to the clothes we wear, we owe it all to the trees. Not only this, trees act as purifiers of air and receptacles of our waste products. Trees have great economic value too. We get fuel, fodder, timber, medicines and numerous other valuable products from the trees. It is, therefore, not surprising that trees were given great importance in our culture, our tradition, our mythology and legends. The entire Panchatantra revolves around forests and its inhabitants. Tulsi plant is always found and worshipped in a traditional home. Pipal tree is revered by all. Neem is valuable as an insecticide, germicide and medicine, in the times when there were no coolers or air conditioners people comforted themselves in the cool shades of mango, neem and other trees during summer heat. The survival of entire wild life depends upon the health and well being of our trees and specially our forests.

Today, however, the forests are in danger. Their survival is at stake as man, in his blind pursuit of wealth and power, is bent upon destroying them. The urgent need today is to save our forests from extinction. For sustaining ecological balance, for environmental and other reasons, it is important that at least one third of our land is covered with forests.

However, today we have less than 20% area under forests and much of it is degraded forest. Over felling of trees, hindering natural process of pollination and germination and diverting land for other purposes have all taken their toll on forests. So, the need of the hour is to work to save existing forests and help in bringing larger area under forests. The need to conserve forests and upgrade them was recognized decades back by the Indian Government.

Subsequently, to promote research in forestry and allied sciences, a Forest Research Institute, and for forest management, an Indian Institute of Forest Management were opened. While Indian Forest Service was organized on an efficient basis by Sir John Strachey, a new orientation was given to it after independence. The need to involve public was felt and so social forestry scheme was launched. The purpose was to make forestry a mass movement. 'One tree for every child', Trees for Eco-development' and numerous other schemes were launched. To provide financial support, Forest Development Boards were set-up. An innovative scheme to involve industries and private parties in afforestation drive was launched under Industrial Plantation. To make use of the waste lands, marginal lands and desert lands, 'energy plantations', fodder plantations' etc. were attempted.

Under DDP, forests were sought to be promoted not only to restore fragile ecological balance but also to provide people with the means of livelihood. Similarly, DPAP was launched with afforestation as its cornerstone.

Despite all such efforts, we find very little tangible result. Forests are still getting cut and degraded and wildlife still being destroyed. Somehow, the awareness that forests are in danger and that we should do something about it has still not reached many of us. And many of us, who know the fact, do not know what to be done about it. Forestry is highly labor intensive primary activity. Unless, people are involved neck deep in the afforestation drive, little progress can be made. Spread of information by mass media, through social workers, in schools and colleges, at work places, all these are required for the drive to become a movement. While most of us know the importance of forests, we take them for granted. Conservation of forests does not mean that they should not be used for economic purposes but should be used efficiently and in a way that does not endanger the ecological balance and does not destroy the home of wild animals. Presently, forests are being used for mainly two purpose— fuelwood and timber—both involve felling trees.

This can be avoided by either developing alternative sources of energy (there are many-solar, biogas etc.), alternative means for construction (CPWD has banned the use of wood in houses) or by growing at least one (if not two) tree for each tree cut. Secondly, new, better means of using forests should be evolved. Sericulture, mushroom cultivation, bee keeping, horticulture, etc. are not only viable but also very profitable alternatives. At the same time, forests should be protected as a system. This means that monocultures are avoided and variety of trees suitable to the local environs be grown.

The question today is not whether or not afforestation but how. Our very survival depends upon how successful we are in our mission. Let us think about future. In the greed for short-term gains, Let us not put our very survival at stake. We all have role to play in this movement. If each one of us grows just one healthy and suitable tree in his life time, the problem will be solved. To misquote Armstrong—It is a small 'ask for each one of us but a giant task for the mankind.

Friendship

Friendship is a relationship that has many dimensions and styles. Friendship can be of between any two or persons and there is no compulsion of age, gender, geography, race, creed or nationality. People living in a house or living in this world are equally to prone to this relationship of friendship. Friendship has no boundaries and no limits.

In life, every one will meet many people who say that they are your friend, but you will make only a few true friends. What is a friend? In the dictionary a friend is defined as one that is not hostile, or one attached to another by affection or esteem, a favoured companion. In my opinion a friend is much more than that. A friend is some one that will stand by you, even during the toughest times. Friendship is about believing in your friends and helping them to achieve all they can or want to do in life. We are there for each other with hugs, advice, kind words, fights, and anger, whatever comes along. When the day ends, we are still friends who have each other no matter what happens.

We all have a desire to have friends. It is what makes us reach out of our shells and take the chance of being hurt. It is not easy figuring out who is a friend and who is not. I believe Divya, to be a true friend. We meet in high school and have known each other for five years. Divya and I have been through many good and hard times together. In addition, we have experienced so many adventures together, such as travelling to Italy and the Caribbean where we shared so many enjoyable adventures. Are friendship has done nothing but grow and continues to do so. We are currently indulgencing in another adventure by living together in Ottawa, and are going to be attending Carleton University in September.

I consider Divya to be a true friend. A true friend is there for you when you need them. To have a true friend is a remarkable thing. To find someone that shares similar interests, who cares about whom you are and what you are doing. A true friend is there for you when you need them. Someone who you are not embarrassed to cry in front of, who you can tell the deepest darkest secrets to and know they will be safe. An old rule of thumb is that a true friend is someone you can call after months or ever years and speak as if not a day had passed. Divya and I have experienced this, we were parted from each other for about a year and half while she was away at her first year university and I moved back to my home India to spend some time with my mom. Once we came in contact again with each other to attend university it was as though we never skipped a beat.

True friendships come along so rarely, and I am so thankful to have met her that we must move past anything that threatens them and see the big picture. Without our friendships, we are indeed lost. Whatever happens, we should always keep our true friends close to our heart. Tell them how much they mean to you. Do not let them slip away. If they do, go out and get them back. The bonds we make during these days will serve to keep us going in the months and years ahead.

Antibiotics

Antibiotics are playing an important role in our society. Sir Alexander Fleming's was a founder of antibiotics through his careful observations of 1928. Without it, many lives would have been in danger due to so many infectious diseases. Antibiotics are chemical substances produced by various species of micro-organisms and other living systems that are capable of inhibiting the growth of killing bacteria and other micro-organisms, in small concentrations. These organisms can be bacteria, viruses, fungi or animals called protozoa. A particular group of these agents is made up of drugs called antibiotics.

Antibiotics can be bacteriostatic (bacteria stopped from multiplying) or bactericidal (bacteria killed). It is believed that antibiotics interfere with the surface of bacteria cells, causing a change in their ability to reproduce. Antibiotics are manufactured in two ways. One of them is natural. At one time, all antibiotics were made from living organisms. This process, known as biosynthesis, is still used in the manufacture of some antibiotics. Other type is synthetic. All penicillin types have an identical chemical nucleus called a ring. The chemical chain that is attached to the ring is different in each type. By changing the molecules of the chain, scientists devise drugs with potentially different effects on different organisms. Some of these drugs are useful in treating infections, some are not.

Pharmaceutical manufacturers now use computer-generated images of the rings and experiment with an endless variety of possible chains. Researchers have developed antibiotics which allow taking the medicine once in 24 hours instead of every few hours. The newer antibiotics are also more effective against a wider range of infections than were earlier drugs. There are dozens of antibiotics. The following are in common use:

Penicillin: The various types of Penicillin's make up a large group of antibacterial antibiotics.

Cephalosporin: These drugs are used for combating deep infections that occur in bones and those resulting from surgery.

Aminoglycoside: These drugs are used to treat tuberculosis, bubonic plague and other infections.

Tetracycline: Tetracyclines are effective against pneumonia, typhus and other bacteria-caused illness but can harm the function of the liver and kidney.

Macrolide: Macrolides are often used in patients who appear to be sensitive to Penicillin.

Polypeptide: The class of antibiotics called Polypeptides is quite toxic (poisonous) and is used mostly on the surface of the skin.

Allergic reactions to antibiotics are usually seen as rashes on the skin, but severe anaemia, stomach disorders and deafness can occasionally result. It was once thought that allergic reactions to antibiotics were frequent and permanent. But, recent studies suggest that many people outgrow their sensitivity or never were allergic. The large numbers of antibiotics that are now available offer a choice of treatment that can avoid allergy-causing drugs.

It is well to remember that all drugs can cause both wanted and unwanted effects on the body. It is a fact that all drugs have the potential to be both beneficial and harmful. Another use of antibiotics is, as additives to the feed of animals. Chickens and beef cattle, can be fed with these additives for better weight gains and to speed their growth.

Current work in antibiotics is largely in the area of viruses. Although some antiviral are available, most have toxic effects so severe that they can be used only in life-threatening diseases where the negative effects are the lesser danger. Preliminary studies, however, are reporting success in the development of safer antiviral drugs and their use should be possible within the near future.

India and Climate Change

The threat of climate change that led to the Framework Convention on Climate Change (FCCC) at Rio, is perceived differently by different countries. This fact has delayed any effective international agreement on how to deal with the problem. In the case of the Montreal Protocol covering ozone-depleting substances, there was a wide consensus and effective action was mobilized quickly. Thus, an understanding of perceptions and positions of different countries makes it easier to explore possibilities of effective action.

Precisely at a time when India is confronted with development imperatives, we will also be severely impacted by climate change. Like other developing countries, several sections of the Indian populace will not be able to buffer themselves from impacts of global warming. With close economic ties to natural resources and climate-sensitive sectors such as agriculture, water and forestry, India may face a major threat, and require serious adaptive capacity to combat climate change. As a developing country, India can little afford the risks and economic backlashes that industrialized nations can. With 27.5% of the population still below the poverty line, reducing vulnerability to the impacts of climate change is essential.

It is in India's interest to ensure that the world moves towards a low carbon future. Many studies have underscored the nation's vulnerability to climate change. With changes in key climate variables, namely temperature, precipitation and humidity, crucial sectors like agriculture and rural development are likely to be affected in a major way.

Impacts are already being seen in unprecedented heat waves,

cyclones, floods, salinization of the coastline and effects on agriculture, fisheries and health.

India is home to a third of the world's poor, and climate change will hit this section of society the hardest. Set to be the most populous nation in the world by 2045, the economic, social and ecological price of climate change will be massive.

The future impacts of climate change, identified by the Government of India's National Communications (NATCOM) in 2004 include:

- Decreased snow cover, affecting snow-fed and glacial systems such as the Ganges and Brahmaputra. 70% of the summer flow of the Ganges comes from melt water.
- Erratic monsoon with serious effects on rain-fed agriculture, peninsular rivers, water and power supply.
- Drop in wheat production by 4-5 million tones, with even a 1°C rise in temperature.
- Rising sea levels causing displacement along one of the most densely populated coastlines in the world, threatened freshwater sources and mangrove ecosystems.
- Increased frequency and intensity of floods. Increased vulnerability of people in coastal, arid and semi-arid zones of the country.
- Studies indicate that over 50% of India's forests are likely to experience shift in forest types, adversely impacting associated biodiversity, regional climate dynamics as well as livelihoods based on forest products.

India stands to lose on too many counts to allow a 'climate-politics-as-usual' scenario. Therefore, positive engagement with global climate negotiations at the next UNFCCC meeting in December 2009 is crucial.

India's Accelerating Emissions

Although not an emitter historically, India currently has one of the fastest growing economies in the world. With a government target of 8% GDP to achieve developmental priorities, a share of one sixth of the global population, and changing consumption patterns, India's emissions are set to increase dramatically.

Growing at an almost breakneck pace, and guzzling coal, gas and oil in large quantities, we are today, the fourth largest emitter of greenhouse gases worldwide. Although our per-capita emissions are among the lowest in the world, our growth rates imply that the past is no predictor of the future. The most recent IPCC report suggests that India will experience the greatest increase in energy and greenhouse gas emissions in the world if it sustains a high annual economic growth rate. The International energy Agency predicts that India will become the third largest emitter of greenhouse gases by as early as 2015.

India imports large quantities of fossil fuels to meet its energy needs, and the burning of fossil fuels alone accounts for 83% of India's carbon dioxide emissions. Nearly 70% of our electricity supply comes from coal.

Although India has maintained its clear economic and social development imperatives, the government recognizes that climate change is a serious problem, and that business as usual is no longer the way forward.

India on Climate Change

India has committed to actively engage in multilateral negotiations in the UNFCCC, in a 'positive and forward-looking manner'. The government recognizes that 'global warming will affect us seriously' but maintains that the 'most important adaptation measure to climate change is development itself'. This has ensured that India's position at the UNFCC has stubbornly remained 'common but differentiated responsibility'. Under the UNFCCC agreement itself, India is not subject to any binding emission reduction targets until the year 2012.

In spite of this guarded stand, India has 'declared' that even as it pursues its social and development objectives, it will not allow its per capita emissions to exceed those of developed countries. The 11th 5-year plan does make headway in reducing energy intensity per unit of GHG by 20 per cent while boosting cleaner and renewable energy.

In June 2008, the Prime minister released the much awaited National Action Plan on Climate Change (NAPCC). The NAPCC outlines a strategy by which India will adapt to climate change, while maintaining a high growth rate, protecting poor and vulnerable sections of society and achieving national growth objectives. It focuses on eight areas intended to deliver maximal benefits to development and climate change (mitigation and adaptation). However, detailed action plans for each mission, and any clear targets are missing from the report.

Although the action plan may be a missed opportunity for leadership on climate change, the good news is that change is coming. Realizing that the market is changing, and not to be left behind in the global race, Indian businesses are beginning to take on climate change as a business issue.

What we need now is for the government of India to capitalize on India's position as a developing giant, take the lead and engage with governments of the world and the private sector for a low-carbon future.

India Education and Employment

Education in India is provided by the public sector as well as the private sector. The control and funding come from three levels: federal, state, and local. Child education is compulsory. The Nalanda University was the oldest university-system of education in the world. Western education became ingrained into Indian society with the establishment of the British Raj.

However, it is disheartening to accept that India is going to experience a paradox of nearly 90 million people joining the workforce but most of them will lack requisite skills and the mindset for productive employment according to a report in DNA. India has about 550 million people under the age of 25 years out of which only 11% are enrolled in tertiary institutions compared to the world average of 23%.

It is unfortunate to note that India education system's failure is leading to another social issue of income inequality. There is a need of certain policies to improve India's education system and reduce inequality.

The really critical aspect of Indian public education system is its low quality. The actual quantity of schooling that children experience and the quality of teaching they receive are extremely insufficient in government schools. A common feature in all government schools is the poor quality of education, with weak infrastructure and inadequate pedagogic attention.

What the government is not realizing right now is that education which is a source of human capital can create wide income inequalities. It will be surprising to see how income inequalities are created within the same group of educated people. Let us see this with the help of an example:

Let us take X be an individual who has had no primary or higher education. His human capital is zero and hence it bears no returns. Let Y be an individual who completed his MBA from S.X Jain college and let Z be an individual who completed his MBA from IIM Ahmadabad. The average rate of return for an MBA student is 7.5% (hypothetical). Y gets a rate of return of 5% and Z gets a rate of return of 10% due to the difference in the reputation and quality of the management school. Let the income of X, Y and Z be 1. In a period of 10 years, X will be having the same income as he does not possess human capital. For the same time period Y will earn an income of (1+0.05)^10=1.63 and Z will earn an income of (1+0.10)^10=2.59.

Now, let's see what happens when the rate of return on human capital doubles. Earnings of X will not change since he does not have any human capital. Now Y is going to earn (1+0.10)^10=2.59 and Z is going to earn (1+0.20)^10=6.19. Flabbergasting! As soon as return on human capital increases proportionately income inequality increases. With return on human capital doubling, Y'S income increases by 59% and Z's income increases by 139%.

The above example just shows the effect of the quality of human capital in income inequality. So if the government does not improve education system particularly in rural areas the rich will become richer and the poor will get poorer.

Hence, it is imperative for the government to correct the blemishes in India's education system which will also be a step towards reducing income inequality.

Certain policy measures need to be taken by the

Government. The basic thrust of government education spending today must surely be to ensure that all children have access to government schools and to raise the quality of education in those schools. One of the ways in which the problem of poor quality of education can be tackled is through common schooling. This essentially means sharing of resources between private and public schools. Shift system is one of the ways through which common schooling can be achieved. The private school can use the resources during the first half of the day and the government school can use it during the second half. It is important to remember that the quality of education is directly linked to the resources available and it is important for the government to improve resource allocation to bring about qualitative changes in the field of education. Common schooling is one of the ways in which government can use limited resources in an efficient way and thus improve resource allocation.

Another reason for poor quality of education is the poor quality of teachers in government schools. Government schools are unable to attract good quality teachers due to inadequate teaching facilities and low salaries. The government currently spends only 3% of its GDP on education which is inadequate and insufficient. To improve the quality of education, the government needs to spend more money from its coffers on education.

Most economists feel that the only panacea to the ills of the public schooling system is the voucher scheme. Under the voucher system, parents are allowed to choose a school for their children and they get full or partial reimbursement for the expenses from the government. But however, the voucher system will further aggravate the problem of poor quality of education in government schools. Such a system will shift resources from government schools to private schools. This will worsen the situation of government schools which are already under-funded. Moreover, if the same amount given as vouchers can be used to build infrastructure in schools then the government can realize economies of scale. For example, The centre for civil society is providing vouchers worth ₹4000 per annum to 308 girls. This means that the total amount of money given as vouchers is ₹ 1232000. If the same amount can be used to construct a school and employ high quality teachers who are paid well then a larger section of the society will enjoy the benefit of education. A school can definitely accommodate a minimum of 1000 students.

The present day education system in India has come a long way and the age old traditions have undergone a makeover to produce an ecosystem that is evolving every single day.

Initiatives like the Right to Education Act have provided an impetus to growth and progress by laying special emphasis on elementary education in India. Combined with policy changes like making child labour illegal the being government is working ensure that the seeds of education are planted in both the rural and less privileged sub-urban areas of the country though there are a number of pressing challenges at hand that hamper the proliferation.

Key Challenges for the Indian Education System

25% of the Indian population is illiterate. Only 7% of the population that goes to school managed to graduate and only 15% of those who enrol manage to make it to high school and achieve a place in the higher education system.

A few reasons why education in India is given less importance in some areas are as follows:

- 80% of schools are managed by the government. Private schools are expensive and out of reach of the poor.
- More hands to earn remains the mentality amongst many families and therefore little kids are set out to fend for the family over going to school to garner an adequate education, in the most literal sense of the word.
- Infrastructure facilities at schools across rural areas and in slums dispense very poor quality of education.
- The teachers are not well qualified and therefore not well paid and therefore are not willing to work hard enough. This has been a classical Catch-22 problem that the government has been trying hard to fight against.

An Overview of the Levels of Education in India

The type of education systems in India can be classified as:

1. **Pre-primary Education in India:** Pre-primary school education in India is not a fundamental right and is divided into two levels – Lower KG (for children between 3–4 years) and Upper KG (for children between 4–5 years).
2. **Primary Education in India:** This serves as the link between primary school and elementary education. However, not much emphasis is laid on this level by the prevailing education system and policies in this regard continue to exist solely on paper.
3. **Elementary Education:** The Government has made elementary education compulsory for children between the age group of years 6 and 14.
4. **Secondary Education in India**: Serves as a link between elementary and higher education in the Indian education setup, which draws a blank again as far as policy is concerned.

5. **Higher Education in India**: Under-graduate and post-graduate level: After completion of secondary education, students can choose fields of their interest and pursue undergraduate and then post-graduate courses.

Curriculum Bodies

Catering to the largerst population in the world is no easy task and as the annals of beureaucracy dictate, there are more than 15 education boards across the country.

While some of them are regional, the more interesting ones are listed below:

The NCERT – Apex Body for curriculum:

As far as school education and its functions are concerned, the National Council of Educational Research and Training takes care of all curriculum related matters. Various schools in the country seek technical assistance from this body.

State Government Boards: Since 80% of the schools in India are managed by the government, this is the board under which the most children in India get enrolled. The Board of Secondary Education across major states has achieved its objectives of developing various systems.

CBSE: The Central Board of Secondary Education which falls under the purview of the Central Government is a board of education for both public and private schools in India.

ICSE: The Council for the Indian School Certificate Examinations Board is a non-governmental and private education board for education in India.

NIOS: Established by the Government of India and the Ministry for Human Resource Development in 1989, the National Institute of Schooling Board aims at providing quality education in rural areas in a inexpensive manner.

Cambridge International Exams/IB: International Baccalaureate or Cambridge International Examinations offer international qualifications to students. This is a recent phenomenon in various parts of the country and is mostly offered by upmarket schools and the like.

Islamic Madrasah Schools: These schools may be either controlled by the state government, run autonomously or may be affiliated with the Darul Uloom Deoband that is in the Sahranpur District of Uttar Pradesh.

While there are a number of drawbacks of the education system in India, a number of efforts are being made to create awareness and action for education in India.

Efforts like the *Sarva Shisksha Abhiyan* aim at making education and good quality of life for today's children possible by providing community owned school systems. Another indicator of a brighter tomorrow is the Right of Children to free and compulsory education. Large investments in the education system truly make us believe that the children of India will get off the streets and start making education their mainstay for a successful life.

Like with most things we are exposed to today, there are two sides to the education system in India – both good and bad which has made it a subject of many essays and a lot many discourses.

Importance of Praying

India is a country that is blessed with several castes, creeds, sects and religions in India. We profess different religions. There are Hindus, Muslims, Sikhs, Christians, Buddhists, Jains and Parsis. All religions teach us to pray to God. Irrespective of our religions, we pray to God, but we pray to God in different ways, at different places and at different times. All regions tell us that we must pray to God, but what is the necessity of praying to God?

God is very kind. He showers His blessing equally on all, whether we pray or do not pray to Him. He has gifted us many things free of cost. He is a great forgiver. He does not punish us for our sins. He forgives our sins committed unknowingly. We must remember Him and Pray to Him to express our thanks.

We must pray to God because God has bestowed us with all the gifts, we possess. We must pray and thank Him for all those favours. He has given us innumerable gifts– Our life, our beautiful earth, the sun, the moon and the starts. All are the wonderful gifts given by God. Prayer is a must to thank and to show our gratitude to God for all the gifts He has bestowed upon us.

Prayer also helps us to face problems in life. Life is full of problems and troubles. It is not smooth sailing. There is a lot of pain, sorrows and sufferings in life. We seek God's help to overcome these problems and troubles. Prayer gives us this help and moral support to face our problems.

Man is a weak and helpless being. He cannot do anything of his own. He loses courage and gives up everything. He loses peace of mind at every step. An accident, sickness or deaths of some beloved are the examples of helplessness of men. On all such occasions he has to take the help of prayer, because it boosts up his confidence.

Prayer is like talking to God as a close Friend or loving Father. When we pray to God, we fell as if God is present with us. We can talk to Him and place our problems before Him.

We beg Him for His blessings. When God is with us, who can cause any harm to us? Prayer means trust in God. It gives us courage and confidence. Prayer binds us with God and brings us nearer to Him.

Prayer is a must because; it gives us strength and courage to face our life problems. It gives us peace of mind, comfort and consolation. Prayer to God is also necessary because, it has magic power. Problems which cannot be solved otherwise, find easy solution in prayer. Such problems get solved automatically by themselves with the magi power of prayer. Disease which are inculpable and cannot be cured with the help of medicines, vanish completely with the magic power of prayer. If we pray earnestly and honestly, God is king enough to shower His blessings. Prayer is the most powerful weapon we can depend upon.

God is present everywhere. There is no place where He is not present. He can come to our aid anywhere we are. Prayer helps us to remember this truth. It removes all unnecessary fears fro our minds. It is the prayer that tells us that God is omnipresent. He must come to our rescue, whenever we are caught in some trouble. We seek His help from the core of our Hearts by prayer.

Prayer is necessary to keep us on the right path, away from the evil ways. If we follow evil ways, we shall go away from God. We shall not be able to communicate with God. We cannot pray to God in the right earnest. God knows everything. We cannot hide anything from Him. He knows even our inner-most thoughts. We cannot bluff Him. God listens to the prayer of only those who are good and noble. We need God's blessings and help at every moment. So we must not be wicked or evil, we must remain good and holy.

Prayer is a must for everyone. We cannot do anything without prayer. It is the most useful means, because more wonderful things can be wrought by prayer than a man can dream of. Prayer is a powerful weapon.

Top Tourist Destinations in India

India is the land of myriad experiences and exotic locales. It is a world of resplendent colours and rich cultural locales, be it magnificent monuments, heritage temples or tombs. The Country's ancient cultural heritage is inextricably linked to its technology driven present existence. The co-existence of a number of religions and cultures, together with an awe-inspiring topography makes it the perfect place for a complete holiday experience.

Tourism in India is the largest service industry, with a contribution of 6.23% to the national GDP and 8.78% of the total employment in India. India witnesses more than 5.5 million annual foreign tourist arrivals and 740 million domestic tourism visits. The tourism industry in India generated about 100 billion US$ in 2008 and that is expected to increase to US$275.5 billion by 2018 at a 9.4% annual growth rate.

In the year 2010, 17.9 million foreign tourists visited India. Majority of foreign tourists come from USA and UK. Maharashtra, Tamil Nadu, Delhi, Uttar Pradesh and Rajasthan are the top 5 states to receive inbound tourists.

Domestic tourism in the same year was massive at 740 million. Andhra Pradesh, Uttar Pradesh, Tamil Nadu and Maharashtra received the big share of these visitors.

Have a look at some of the most impressive tourist destinations in India.

Leh, Jammu & Kashmir

This mountain town in Ladakh is quickly rising to the top of must-visit lists. Not surprising when you consider the sheer natural beauty of the place.

The towering Himalayas supply a dramatic backdrop and plenty of opportunity for adrenaline junkies to get their fix.

Rock climbing, white-water rafting and skiing are all on offer, and if you're looking for something a little tamer, short trekking jaunts can be arranged.

For a glimpse into the town's culture and rich history, visit the Shey Palace and the many Buddhist monasteries.

Varanasi, Uttar Pradesh

One of most significant religious centres of Hinduism, Varasani needs to visited to be believed. Bustling with devotees, sadhus, tourists and locals, the place is teeming with sights that are uniquely Indian.

The temples and *ghats* (steps leading to the Ganga) with thousands of devotees performing religious rituals and dotted with Hindu priests performing rites is quite a sight to behold.

The Vishwanath Temple, Sarnath Deer Park and the Ram Nagar Fort are worth a visit. Also the Panchganaga, Dasaswamedh and Kedar ghats offer a great slice of Varanasi life.

Manali, Himachal Pradesh

One of India's prettiest hill stations, Manali has long been a honeymooner's paradise. But the little town nestled in the mighty Himalayas offers plenty of entertainment for adventure seekers.

The Beas river has whitewater rafting and there's skiing,

trekking, paragliding and zorbing to be done all along the hilly terrain nearby.

Rohtang Pass has mesmerizing views of the great mountains, the Vashisht hot water springs has bathhouses for visitors to soak in the bubbling water and then there are large and small waterfalls at short drives all around Manali. So make sure you pack your outdoor gear.

Darjeeling, West Bengal

This little tea town came into prominence during the British Raj. It was then that Darjeeling was developed as a hill station and tea plantation area, thanks to its cooler temperatures.

Today, Darjeeling's tea estates are world-renowned, but there's more to it than its picturesque rolling hills sheathed in green.

Nestled in the Lesser Himalayas, Darjeeling offers breath-taking views of the great mountains including Mt Everest.

Tiger Hill, at an altitude of 2,590 metres gives visitors a glimpse of the Kanchen Junga range. Plus there's plenty of rock-climbing and trekking opportunities for the adventurous.

The ropeway and cable car rides, the natural history museum, the zoological parks and botanical gardens all give tourists a flavour of the natural wealth of the Himalayas.

The Darjeeling Himalayan Railway with its toy train is also worth a visit, being named a World Heritage Site.

Jaisalmer, Rajasthan

The 'Golden City' has long been a tourist hotspot thanks to its royal history. The desert town boasts of the Jaisalmer Fort (that houses the Raj Mahal), a number of *havelis*, the most impressive being the Amar Sagar, Patwon-ki-Haveli and Nathmalji-ki-Haveli, and ornate Jain temples.

Tourists can explore the Thar desert perched atop camels, visit the Desert National Park for a gander at the fauna, or the Akal Wood Fossil Park. Of course, there's plenty of shopping to be done for traditional Rajasthani art, clothes and jewellery.

Bengaluru, Karnataka

This buzzing metro might be one of the most recognized Indian cities abroad, but the 'Garden City' had plenty going for it long before it became an IT hub.

Bengaluru offers a blend of the old and the new and won't disappoint. The Bangalore Palace and Summer Palace are a glimpse into the city's royal past and the imposing Vidhana Soudha structure an example of its prosperous present.

There are plenty of ancient religious centres, such as St. Mary's Basilica, St Patric's Church, the Masjid-e-Khadria and Shri Nimishamba Devi Temple.

Younger tourists will enjoy the plentiful shopping at the many malls, all offering the biggest brands, and the thriving nightlife complete with pubs and lounge bars.

Agra, Uttar Pradesh

Agra needs no introduction. The timeless Taj Mahal makes it to almost every must-visit list, and deservedly so. The white marble structure and the sprawling campus around it are simply magnificent.

And while the Taj will be the highlight of any visit to the city, there are quite a few other architectural delights the city offers visitors.

The Agra Fort is another majestic construction, bearing

plenty of evidence of the regalia of Mughal times. Some other attractions include the Sikandra complex, Swami Bagh and Itmad-ud-Daulah's Tomb.

Mumbai, Maharashtra

The country's commercial capital, Mumbai's rhythm needs to be experience to be believed. Fast-paced and constantly on the go, the city has something for everyone.

Colonial architecture, diverse cuisine and plenty of entertainment options are just some of what's in store. Shopping is a tourist's delight, and the nightlife while have you partying away. Some of the must-visits are the Gateway of India and the Taj Mahal hotel opposite, Juhu Beach and Chowpatty for the fast food; and Bandra for the shopping.

There's Film City for a glimpse of some Bollywood stars and drop by one of the many religious sites for some spiritual upliftment. Mt. Mary's Church, Haji Ali mosque, and the ISCKON temple are just some of the crowd-pullers.

Jaipur, Rajasthan

It is Jaipur's rich history and culture that have made it one of the three major tourist centres in the state.

Imposing forts, awe-inspiring palaces and exquisite temples are all there and plenty of them. Visit the Jaigarh and Amber Forts and catch the Amber sound and light show for a glimpse of the city's history. The City Palace and Jal Mahal are must-sees. There are also a number of gardens that are perfect for long walks in beautiful surrounds.

Munnar, Kerala

This sleepy little tea town is best known (apart from its tea blends) for its rolling green hills and scenic beauty.

There's not much to do in town except for relax and take in the beauty of the place, but there are a number of attractions short distances away.

Some of these include the Atukkad Falls, Mattupetti Dam, Kundala Lake and the Eravikullam National Park, where you can spot the endangered Nilgiri Thar. There are also elephant tours that can be organized from the town for the more adventurous.

Hampi, Karnataka

The ancient ruins of Hampi have been drawing tourists for decades thanks to the legendary tales of the prosperity under the Vijayanagar Empire.

The ruins have been recognized as a World Heritage Site and continue to delight visitors with its stark, rocky contrast to the surrounding green.

Apart from the ruins, there are a number of significant temples that include the Virupaksha Temple, the Hazara Rama Temple and the Vitthala Temple. And if it's stunning scenery you're after, hike up the Matanga Hill for panoramic views of the city.

Udaipur, Rajasthan

This Rajasthani city is tourist magnet thanks to its serene lakes and beautiful palaces.

Topping the list of must-see spots is the Udaipur City Palace, with its impeccably maintained gardens, luxurious halls and chambers.

The Pichola and Fateh Sagar both offer a variety of attractions for tourists and the Saheliyon-ki-Badi has opulent gardens and fountains that are definitely worth a viewing.

As with most Rajasthani cities and towns, there is plenty of shopping here. So if you're looking for traditional arts, jewellery or clothing, Udaipur is just the place to go.

New Delhi

There is plenty to see and do in the country's capital, so make sure you draw up an itinerary.

The imposing Red Fort and sprawling complex of Humayun's Tomb are a definite must-see, as are the Qutub Minar and Baha'i Temple. Visit Rajpath, from Rashtrapati Bhavan to India Gate to take in the majesty of the place.

Drop by Connaught Place for some great shopping and dining and Chandni Chowk for a true Delhi experience.

Srinagar, Jammu and Kashmir

Once a very popular holiday destination, political conflict in recent years has lost the city much of its tourism.

But the beauty of the place still remains, and travellers are sure to catch some beautiful scenery and delicious Kashmiri culinary delights on a trip there.

The Mughal Gardens, Shalimar Bagh and Pari Mahal are well-worth a visit.

Take a shikara ride on the Dal Lake for some peace and tranquility and shop for exquisite Pashmina shawls and Kashmiri rugs and carpets in the city.

Shimla, Himachal Pradesh

Long been a honeymoon paradise, the capital city is quaint and very picturesque. The cool climes in the summer months are a welcome relief and the snowy cold months provide for plenty of winter activity.

Some of the attractions within the city include the Jakhu Temple, Christ Church, Viceregal Lodge and a stroll on Mall road. The hilly terrain also offers plenty of trekking opportunities and in the winters there's ice skating as well.

Goa

Now this one's a no-brainer. No Indian holiday list could be considered complete without this beach paradise.

This former Portuguese colony has something for everyone — temples and churches galore for the culture vultures; pubs and bars for the party animals; restaurants that boast just about every cuisine under the sun; hotels and resorts that offers every activity you can think of,so you don't really need to leave the premises; and of course the beautiful beaches.

Some attractions are the weekly flea market at Anjuna; the pristine beaches in South Goa; the Doodhsagar waterfalls and the many temples and churches that dot this state. Infantaria and Souza Lobo are great for Goan cuisine and continental delights.

A word of advice, the monsoon is not the best time to visit. Most of the beaches are shutdown due to rough seas and the hotels follow suit. The roads will be waterlogged making getting around difficult and most tourist attractions close their doors.

Pune, Maharashtra

Often called the cultural capital of the state, Pune is where the Marathi film industry is based and also where many esteemed centres of higher learning have been established.

The city has 4 museums that tourists can visit including the Raja Dinkar Kelkar Museum, the National War Museum, and palaces such as Shaniwar Wada and the Aga Khan Palace.

Adventure seekers should drop by the Pataleshwar Caves, the Bhimashankar Sanctuary or trek up one of the many nearby forts.

Rishikesh, Uttarakhand

Another important centre of Hinduism, Rishikesh lies along the Ganga river and the Char Dham Yatra, one of the faith's most holy pilgrimages, typically begins here.

Apt from its religious significance, it is also a major centre for yoga and the town is dotted with yoga and meditation schools.

For travellers looking a little adventure can opt for whitewater rafting, kayaking on the river and rappelling, trekking and even bungee jumping along the Himalayas nearby.

Hyderabad, Andhra Pradesh

One of the country's rapidly growing IT hubs, this capital city also boasts a rich cultural heritage going back many centuries.

The famed Charminar and Golconda Fort are big tourist draws and the market around Charminar is great for a bargain. Another architectural gems include the Falaknuma Palace and Mecca Masjid.

The Hussain Sagar and Sharmipet lakes and the gardens and parks nearby all present wonderful picnic opportunities. Of course, there are numerous mosques and temples to not only seek some spiritual upliftment but also to feast your eyes on.

And while your travelling the length and breadth of the city, make sure to load up on plenty of Hyderabadi biryani, you won't regret it!

Kolkata, West Bengal

Often called the cultural capital of the country, Kolkata has a lot to offer tourists who are open to new experiences.

The Victoria Memorial and Birla Planetarium are definite must-sees as are the famous Howrah Bridge and Tagore House (where the great poet was born).

Of course one of the highlights is the food. Drop by Chowringhee Lane for a taste of the street food and make sure you're not on a diet when you come to Kolkata, because turning down the juicy Bengali sandesh would simply be a shame.

Chennai, Tamil Nadu

The state's capital city, Chennai is a bustling metropolis, and offers visitors plenty to do and see. The Marina Beach is the most popular of the beaches, while Edward Elliot's Beach is quieter just as scenic.

There are plenty of old churches, temples and mosques to visit. There's also the Arinjar Anna Zoological Park and Guindy National Park for nature lovers and the Pondy Bazaar and Ranganathan Street for those looking to test their bargaining skills.

Dharamsala, Himachal Pradesh

One of the most popular centres of Buddhism, the little town draws a number of celebrity tourists every year.

McLeod Ganj, a suburb within the town, is home to the Dalai Lama and is a major tourist draw. While actually meeting or even seeing the spiritual leader is a tough ask, most tourists try their luck when they visit the place.

If luck isn't on your side, there are a number of other

tourist attractions in and around town to make it well worth the trip.

The Bhagsunag Falls and Pong Dam lake are ideal for picnics. Monasteries and temples dot the town and most are open to tourists.

For those looking for a thrill try the paragliding at Bir or the many treks that start from town. There are also plenty of meditation and rejuvenation centres if you're looking for a little peace and tranquility.

Puducherry

A quiet little union territory has an interesting history, being the largest of the erstwhile French colonies in India. French is still widely understood here and the architecture and eating spots still continue with the cultural influences.

The town moves along at a relaxed paced and there's not much to do besides walking around taking in the environs so different from any other place in the country.

Some of the popular tourist spots are the beaches (Paradise and Auro), the Aurobindo Ashram, and the Boat House.

There are also plenty of places to get some great French and European cuisine, so if you're in the mood to experiment; this is the place for you!

Amritsar, Punjab

The spiritual centre of Sikhism, the Golden Temple, is situated at Amritsar and draws tens of thousands of devotees and tourists every year.

The temple has a sprawling complex with the central building housing the Harmandir Sahib situated in the middle of the Amrit Sarovar pool.

Apart from the temple, there are a few other places of interest as well. The Jallianwala Bagh, where over 1570 unarmed people were killed by British Indian Army soldiers, still stands and a memorial has been erected in remembrance. The Summer Palace and Mata Temple are both worth a visit as well.

Visitors can also travel to the Wagah border (27 km away), where there is a flag raising ceremony on both the India and Pakistan border every day.

Kodaikanal, Tamil Nadu

Nested in the forested Palani hills, Kodai offers scenic lakes, waterfalls, beautiful valley views and observation points galore.

Some of the must-visit spots include the Berijam Lake (where special permission is required before tourists can visit), the Kodai Lake (for day picnics and boating) and the sprawling Bryant Park.

According to World Travel and Tourism Council, India will be a tourism hotspot from 2009–2018, having the highest 10-year growth potential. Despite short- and medium-term setbacks, such as shortage of hotel rooms, tourism revenues are expected to surge by 42% from 2007 to 2017. India's 5,000 years of history, its length, breadth and the variety of geographic features make its tourism basket large and varied. It presents heritage and cultural tourism along with medical, business and sports tourism. India has a growing medical tourism sector.

Importance of School Magazines

The school magazine is no more a new thing to us. Now-a-days many schools have magazines of their own. Formerly, very few schools had such magazines.

A school magazine is a periodical. School publishes it. The students maintain it with the help of their teachers. It contains essays, Poems and articles. They are written by students in Hindi or in English.

How is Differs from Other Magazines?

The school magazine is different from other magazines. Its circulation is limited to students only. It is now written for the public. Hence it has nothing for the interest of the general public. It generally contains sporting news. It tells about the previous results. It has the name of those who bought frame to the institution.

The school magazine has many advantages. First it teaches students how to write. Students are fond of reading by nature. Hence they avoid writing work. To contribute articles to the magazine they have to write something. For their magazine they have to read and write regularly.

Secondly, the school magazine encourages the students to carry on their studies with great energy. They take part in games to see their names in the school magazine. Each school magazine has statements about the progress of the students. It tells about the prizes, the medals they win. So those who are eager to see their names in the magazine, must work hard at their books. They must do their best on the playground.

Thirdly, the school magazine brings the students in close touch with one another. The writers read other books to increase their knowledge. Again they learn to think for themselves. Their thinking increases their reasoning power. A regular contribution to the magazine improves their art of writing. It gives them to command on the language.

Fourthly, the students lean the value of cooperation for the success of the magazine. A good spirit of competition comes among the students. The essay written by teachers, have many practical suggestions for the students. The students learn the art of writing from the writings of their worthy teachers.

How is it Managed?

A school magazine is conducted by the teachers and the students. In many schools a senior teacher is the editor and a student of the top class is the assistant editor. In many schools, the students are editors, but they are advised in all matters by a senior teacher. The articles for the magazine are written by both the teachers and the students. The students send their articles to the editor. But each and every article is not published. The articles are selected by the editor and the assistant editor. They are corrected and then published in the magazine.

Globalization and India

Globalization is the new buzzword that has come to dominate the world since the nineties of the last century. Till the nineties the process of globalization of the Indian economy was constrained by the barriers to trade and investment liberalization of trade, investment and financial flows initiated in the nineties has progressively lowered the barriers to competition and hastened the pace of globalization.

India had the distinction of being the world's largest economy in the beginning of the Christian era, as it accounted for about 32.9% share of world GDP and about 32.5% of the world population. The goods produced in India had long been exported to far off destinations across the world. Therefore, the concept of globalization is hardly new to India.

India opened up the economy in the early nineties following a major crisis that led by a foreign exchange crunch that dragged the economy close to defaulting on loans. The response was a slew of Domestic and external sector policy measures partly prompted by the immediate needs and partly by the demand of the multilateral organizations. The new policy regime radically pushed forward in favour of amore open and market oriented economy.

Major measures initiated as a part of the liberalization and globalization strategy in the early nineties included scrapping of the industrial licensing regime, reduction in the number of areas reserved for the public sector, amendment of the monopolies and the restrictive trade practices act, start of the privatization programme, reduction in tariff rates and change over to market determined exchange rates.

Over the years there has been a steady liberalization of the current account transactions, more and more sectors opened up for foreign direct investments and portfolio investments facilitating entry of foreign investors in telecom, roads, ports, airports, insurance and other major sectors.

The Indian tariff rates reduced sharply over the decade from a weighted average of 72.5% in 1991-92 to 24.6 in 1996-97.Though tariff rates went up slowly in the late nineties it touched 35.1% in 2001-02. India is committed to reduced tariff rates. Peak tariff rates are to be reduced to be reduced to the minimum with a peak rate of 20%, in another 2 years most non-tariff barriers have been dismantled by March 2002, including almost all quantitative restrictions.

The Global India

The liberalization of the domestic economy and the increasing integration of India with the global economy have helped step up GDP growth rates, which picked up from 5.6% in 1990-91 to a peak level of 77.8% in 1996-97. Growth rates have slowed down since the country has still be able to achieve 5-6% growth rate in three of the last six years. Though growth rates has slumped to the lowest level 4.3% in 2002-03 mainly because of the worst droughts in two decades the growth rates are expected to go up close to 70% in 2003-04. A Global comparison shows that India is now the fastest growing just after China.

This is major improvement given that India is growth rate in the 1970's was very low at 3% and GDP growth in countries like Brazil, Indonesia, Korea, and Mexico was more than twice that of India. Though India's average annual growth rate almost doubled in the eighties to 5.9% it was still lower than the growth rate in China, Korea and Indonesia. The pick up in GDP growth has helped improve India's global position. Consequently India's position in the global economy has improved from the 8th position in 1991 to 4th place in 2001. When GDP is calculated on a purchasing power parity basis.

Globalization and Poverty

Globalization in the form of increased integration though trade and investment is an important reason why much progress has been made in reducing poverty and global inequality over recent decades. But it is not the only reason for this often unrecognized progress, good national polices, sound institutions and domestic political stability also matter.

Despite this progress, poverty remains one of the most serious international challenges we face up to 1.2 billion of the developing world 4.8 billion people still live in extreme poverty.

But the proportion of the world population living in poverty has been steadily declining and since 1980 the absolute number of poor people has stopped rising and appears to have fallen in recent years despite strong population growth in poor countries. If the proportion living in poverty had not fallen since 1987 alone a further 215million people would be living in extreme poverty today.

India has to concentrate on five important areas or things to follow to achieve this goal. The areas like technological entrepreneurship, new business openings for small and medium enterprises, importance of quality management, new prospects in rural areas and privatisation of financial institutions. The manufacturing of technology and management of technology are two different significant areas in the country.

There will be new prospects in rural India. The growth of Indian economy very much depends upon rural participation in the global race. After implementing the new economic policy the role of villages got its own significance because of its unique outlook and branding methods. For example food processing and packaging are the one of the area where new entrepreneurs can enter into a big way. It may be organized in a collective way with the help of co-operatives to meet the global demand.

Understanding the current status of globalization is necessary for setting course for future. For all nations to reap the full benefits of globalization it is essential to create a level playing field. President Bush's recent proposal to eliminate all tariffs on all manufactured goods by 2015 will do it. In fact it may exacerbate the prevalent inequalities. According to this proposal, tariffs of 5% or less on all manufactured goods will be eliminated by 2005 and higher than 5% will be lowered to 8%. Starting 2010 the 8% tariffs will be lowered each year until they are eliminated by 2015.

GDP Growth rate

The Indian economy is passing through a difficult phase

caused by several unfavourable domestic and external developments; Domestic output and Demand conditions were adversely affected by poor performance in agriculture in the past two years. The global economy experienced an overall deceleration and recorded an output growth of 2.4% during the past year growth in real GDP in 2001-02 was 5.4% as per the Economic Survey in 2000-01. The performance in the first quarter of the financial year is5.8% and second quarter is 6.1%.

Export and Import

India's Export and Import in the year 2001-02 was to the extent of 32,572 and 38,362 million respectively. Many Indian companies have started becoming respectable players in the International scene. Agriculture exports account for about 13 to 18% of total annual of annual export of the country. In 2000-01 Agricultural products valued at more than US $ 6million were exported from the country 23% of which was contributed by the marine products alone. Marine products in recent years have emerged as the single largest contributor to the total agricultural export from the country accounting for over one fifth of the total agricultural exports. Cereals (mostly basmati rice and non-basmati rice), oil seeds, tea and coffee are the other prominent products each of which accounts for nearly 5 to 10% of the country's total agricultural exports.

India's Position in Global Integration

India clearly lags in globalization. Number of countries have a clear lead among them China, large part of east and far east Asia and eastern Europe. Let's look at a few indicators how much we lag.

- Over the past decade FDI flows into India have averaged around 0.5% of GDP against 5% for China 5.5% for

Brazil. Whereas FDI inflows into China now exceeds US $ 50 billion annually. It is only US $ 4billion in the case of India.

- Consider global trade – India's share of world merchandise exports increased from .05% to .07% over the past 20 years. Over the same period China's share has tripled to almost 4%.
- India's share of global trade is similar to that of the Philippines an economy 6 times smaller according to IMF estimates. India under trades by 70-80% given its size, proximity to markets and labour cost advantages.
- It is interesting to note the remark made last year by Mr. Bimal Jalan, Governor of RBI. Despite all the talk, we are now where ever close being globalized in terms of any commonly used indicator of globalization. In fact we are one of the least globalized among the major countries - however we look at it.
- As Amartya Sen and many other have pointed out that India, as a geographical, politico-cultural entity has been interacting with the outside world throughout history and still continues to do so. It has to adapt, assimilate and contribute. This goes without saying even as we move into what is called a globalized world which is distinguished from previous eras from by faster travel and communication, greater trade linkages, denting of political and economic sovereignty and greater acceptance of democracy as a way of life.

Consequences

The implications of globalization for a national economy are many. Globalization has intensified interdependence and competition between economies in the world market. This is reflected in Interdependence in regard to trading in goods and services and in movement of capital. As a result domestic economic developments are not determined entirely by domestic policies and market conditions. Rather, they are influenced by both domestic and international policies and economic conditions. It is thus clear that a globalizing economy, while formulating and evaluating its domestic policy cannot afford to ignore the possible actions and reactions of policies and developments in the rest of the world. This constrained the policy option available to the government which implies loss of policy autonomy to some extent, in decision-making at the national level.

Terrorism in India is a World Problem

The terror attack in Mumbai was condemned severely by various governments across the world. What was the effect of this attack?

Well, financially India lost ₹ 50, 000 crores and the foreign inflow of funds had reduced which included the tourism that was affected to a great extent because of this and an article said Taj on which the attack was done has to shell out ₹ 500 crores to bring back the lost beauty but on top of this we have lost the important element which is the precious human lives. There were some who did a brave act including Major Unni Krishnan and NSG Chief who lost their lives in order to protect innocent tourists.

Terrorism is something which all over the world is a major problem at the moment. Its effects are very much that it can deteriorate a country's economy and can cause between the countries. Terrorists were not born but they were made in the name of religion. None of the religion preaches terrorism nor ask the followers to take the lives of other people but it was preached by wrong leaders and innocent people fall as a prey and lose their lives and kill other people as well.

Terrorism is in different forms in various countries. In Somalia, it is done by pirates where they hijack lot of ships every now and then and get a hefty ransom because of which UNO has asked the member countries to counter attack this by sending their respective force. India has been doing this for a long time wherein Indian Navy has done a great job having prevented lot of ships being hijacked. China is sending its ships soon to that region. In Afghanistan, it was in the name of Taliban who almost ruined their own country. In Iraq, it was in the name of one dictator in the name of Saddam Hussein who is no more but the effect he has created in his own country, will take a decade at least for that country to recover from its current position.

We saw the brutal attack on Twin Tower on September 11 in USA and did we not cry even though we were in different country. We saw how people struggled and lost their lives right in front of our eyes and could do nothing which eventually led to attack in Afghanistan by USA to demolish Mulla Omar's regime. If USA would have done this earlier, they wouldn't have lost their own people and again on the other hand at the present moment they are funding Pakistan for various causes including purchasing armaments having known the fact that renowned theorists like Dawood Ibrahim are very much based there. They haven't done anything to curb these people who only made an attack on Taj and killed the people of US and UK. We can't blame the Government of US or UK entirely because British Prime Minister Mr. Gordon Brown has condemned Pakistan and said it is done by them. Now people of US should join together to pressure their own Government to act against terrorists based or camping in Pakistan because it is only us, the common people who can make this happen.

The attack on our own Indian Parliament was also one which again checked our patience. We were always united and doing action like these will make us even more unite and fight more strongly than ever against it.

Terrorism affects innocent people because people in Bangalore clearly witnessed the effect in UK bombing where in a Doctor was added as a Prime Suspect just because he is a Muslim and finally he was relieved after he proved himself as being innocent. There are many cases like this across the globe for years together.

Terrorists don't understand that by acting in the name of terrorism, they are bringing disgrace to their own religion and at the same time ruining their own country and people and when they are no more, hardly they could realize the damage they have done and if we have another life or the so called Spirits, these people will realize and make this world a safe and a peaceful place to live.

Euthanasia– Mercy Killing

Euthanasia means as an action which aims at taking the life of another at the latter's expressed request. It concerns an action of which death is the purpose and the result. This definition applies only to voluntary euthanasia and excludes the non-voluntary or involuntary euthanasia, the killing of a patient without the patient's knowledge or consent. Some call this 'life-terminating treatment.'

Euthanasia can be either active or passive. Passive euthanasia allows one to die by withholding or withdrawing life supporting means. This is a tricky area because ordinary and extraordinary means of supporting life come into the picture. Ordinary means such as nutrition and hydration are never to be withheld since they are one's basic right in order to survive. However, one is not obliged to use extraordinary or 'disproportionate' means to sustain life. Due to complexity, each situation needs to be looked at individually when discussing extraordinary means. However, as a rule, one can discontinue 'medical procedures that are burdensome, dangerous, extraordinary, or disproportionate to the expected outcome.' One cannot intend death by withdrawing or withholding treatment, but should, however, obey God and let one die a natural death. To withdraw a treatment as a condition worsens is letting one die and not a direct killing. In this case, it is the disease that is killing and not the one who withdraws the treatment.

Active euthanasia or 'mercy killing' is the direct intentional killing of a patient with either their consent (voluntary), without their consent when impossible (non-voluntary), or without consent but not sought (involuntary). Advocates of this murder have covered their ears to the command of the Lord: Thou shall not kill! The goal is to eliminate or relieve suffering by an evil means of death. Many patients' are in immense suffering and may be led to choose death as the answer by these' doctors', friends or relatives. The culpability for the patient, in these cases may be lessened, but, this act of killing can never be justified.

These patients, whether having an incurable disease, being elderly, or suffering in other ways, are crying out for help and love. Palliative care, not death, is the answer. Medical personnel, friends and family must reach out and comfort the afflicted. Suffering and pain is manageable, especially today, with so many medicines and treatments available. Pain killers can be prescribed as long as there is no danger or intention of death. Consciousness of the patient is strongly encouraged, so that if dying, one may prepare to accept to meet God.

We cannot do whatever to our bodies, since they are not our own. God made us and knows what we need here on earth, so that we, someday, may enter into eternity. If Christ endured immense suffering, then why do we expect any less? We are called to be imitations of Christ and to share in His Passion. Is my life really mine? 'If we live, we are responsible to the Lord, and when we die we are responsible to the Lord. Both in life and death we belong to the Lord.' God has a plan and each human person having an eternal destiny has a dignity. God, being the author of life, alone has the right to create and destroy life. No human person has this right to take innocent human life, no matter how one tries to justify it. Thou shall not kill is still a command and not a suggestion, as many seem to believe.

There are many reasons why Euthanasia is gravely immoral some of which have already been discussed. Suffering has many benefits, especially suffering in the last days of one's life. In addition to sharing in Christ's Passion, one may find peace in God, reconciliation with family and friends and acceptance of death. One also may be undergoing temporal punishment here on earth through suffering; a sort 0 'purgatory on earth'. There are many benefits and advantages to suffering. However in a pragmatic society as ours, we tend to look past the positives and see only the negative side. This type of reasoning has led many to see death as the answer suffering, regardless of the consequences.

Euthanasia whether active or passive is immoral and contrary to God's law Within passive euthanasia, what is considered extraordinary means of sustaining life may not always be clear, but ordinary means such as hydration and nutrition must be provided. We must look past the suffering in this world and look towards eternal home with God. As humans we cannot always see the answers and for that reason, is not we to decide about the death of a human being, God has not given us authority. We must also ask ourselves concerning euthanasia; where will it end: we allow the elderly or incurable to be assisted in suicide, what other groups will give this 'right'. Will the handicapped or mentally retarded be next? Will teenage who are the leading age group of suicide; also have this 'right to die'?

The answer rests in our hands. If we continue to disrespect human life and its creator, God, then well destroy ourselves. A right is a moral claim and since we do not have a claim on death which itself has a claim on us, we cannot act for the right we don't have. Mother Teresa was right when she said that "if a mother can kill her own child, is there to stop you and me from killing each other?' There is no way to stop culture of death, unless, we get back to God's law and speak out, boldly, against horrors and injustices of the day!

We must be wary of those who are too willing to end the lives of the elderly and the ill. If we ever decide that a poor quality of life justifies ending that life have taken a step down a slippery slope that places all of us in danger. There difference between allowing nature to take its course and actively assisting The call for euthanasia surfaces in our society periodically, as it is doing now the guise of 'death with dignity' or assisted suicide. Euthanasia is a concept, it seems to me that am in direct conflict with a religious and ethical tradition in which the human race is presented with a blessing and a curse, life and death, and we are instructed.

I believe 'euthanasia' lies outside the commonly held life

centered valued of the West and cannot be allowed without incurring great, social and personal tragedy. This is not merely an intellectual conundrum. This issue involves actual human beings at risk.

Pollution and Dimming Sun

A blanket of smog hanging over India means the country is getting less and less sunlight, warn researchers. But this phenomenon, known as 'solar dimming' may also protect against global warning.

India is getting about 5% less sunlight than it did 20 years ago, according to a study by Padma Kumari and colleagues at the Indian Institute of Tropical Meteorology in Pune. They studied data from the India Meteorological Department, measuring differences in solar radiation at 12 stations across India between 1981 and 2004.

They found that the amount of solar radiation reaching India's land mass dropped on average by 0.86 watts per square metre each year. The decrease was greater during the 1990s than the 1980s, and on average corresponded to a 5% drop in sunshine over the two decades.

India is losing out on sunshine because a cloud of tiny air-borne particles released by the nation's industries hovers above the subcontinent, blocking light from reaching the Earth.

Masked Warming

Similar dimming has been caused by Western nations too. The smog produced by the US and Europe during the 20th century spread worldwide and was responsible for a phase of 'global dimming'. But when the West cleared up its smog pollution in the 1980s and 1990s, as smog pollution in India was increasing, clearer skies returned. Researchers have described this as 'global brightening'. According to research published in February 2007 by Martin Wild of the Institute for Atmospheric and Climate Science in Switzerland, this global brightening was accompanied by an accelerated rise in global temperatures.

Similarly, Kumari and colleagues believe that the real degree to which India is being warmed by greenhouse gas emissions is being masked by the cooling effect of the smog. Looking at temperature records since the 1980s, they found that maximum and minimum temperatures have both increased, but to different extents.

New Phase

Maximum temperatures, which occur during the day and are driven by sunshine, have risen by just 0.04°C because of the protective effect of the smog.

Meanwhile minimum, night-time temperatures, which are independent of sunshine, have risen by a much greater 0.31°C.

The researchers also found that solar dimming over India was lessened during the monsoon season because the torrential rains brought the fine particles back down to Earth, allowing more sunshine to get through.

Other Asian countries are also likely to be experiencing solar dimming. Preliminary data that Wild and colleagues have from China suggests it is getting less and less sun as well because of rising particle pollution linked to industrialization.

So will the rising smog over India and China bring about a new phase of global dimming? 'There are good chances there indeed,' says Wild.

Can India Become a Superpower?

A potential superpower is a state or a political and economic entity that is speculated to be, or to be in the process of becoming, a superpower at some point in the 21st century. Presently, it is widely considered that only the United States currently fulfills the criteria to be considered a superpower. States most commonly mentioned as being potential superpowers are Brazil, China, the European Union (a supranational entity), India and Russia, based on a variety of factors.

Several media publications and academics have discussed the Republic of India's potential of becoming a superpower. Is India really shining? Is it really on the path of becoming a superpower? Optimistic Indians would assert an affirmation but it is time one had a reality check India is surely marching ahead, but are all the Indians marching ahead or is it just a small fraction of the population doing so? India can surely boast of a growth rate of around 8-9 per cent, but one needs to ask if this growth is trickling down to the lower strata of the populace.

Sixty three years ago in 1947 when India got independence, the question then asked was 'will India survive'? Today, India's economic profile has changed. At over a trillion dollars, it is a force to reckon with not just in Asia but in the entire world. With its new currency symbol to be internationalized soon, India now flexes its financial muscle.

Soon after independence our nation was in turmoil. Assassination of Mahatma Gandhi, tragic partition rendering millions of people homeless, tribal invasion in J&K coupled with problem of consolidation of five hundred princely States, to build a new nation was a mammoth task . After going through different phases of lows and highs, the doubtful query 'will India survive' has been replaced by more hopeful query, 'will India become a superpower'?

Today India is recognized as an emerging powerhouse by the world community. From a nation known to the world as a country of snake charmers to a frontline developing nation, image of our country has undergone a dramatic change. The pace leading to full transformation may be slow but consistency will lead to the desired goal. The key to the extraordinary resilience lies in India's stable and successful democratic institution. India, a home of several religions and several hundred spoken languages is a garland of multitude of diverse communities woven together in a common thread of democracy. Unlike other European nations whose unity is based on a common language and largely a common faith, India presents a picture of unity in diversity. With multiple problems faced by the nation right from its birth, the survival of democracy in India was always in doubt. Despite abstruse dislike and mistrust between the two major communities of the nation, India has emerged as multicultural democracy.

With bold economic reforms India's GDP is on a sustained growth path. India has become third largest economy in Asia to keep its high rate of growth. Despite the growth story, India has yet to cross over many plateaus before it becomes a superpower in league with big nations. I shall discuss here some of the core issues that if not attended to with strong political will and time bound action may rock the boat of country's economic rejuvenation.

Escalating Population

India is second most populous country in the world, with over

1,210,193,422 people more than a sixth of world's population. Already containing 17.31 per cent of the world population, India is projected to be most populous country by 2025 surpassing China. India occupies 2.4 per cent of the world's land and supports 17.5 per cent of world's population. It seems the Govt has stopped all efforts to control the population explosion. Fearing public unrest and possible loss of vote bank, after Sanjay Gandhi the successive Governments abandoned family planning programmes; if at all some programme is being executed it is only as tokenism without political will.

Increasing Unemployment

India is facing massive problem of unemployment. The incidence of unemployment is much higher in urban areas than in rural areas. The incidence of unemployment amongst the educated is higher than the overall unemployment. Economic reforms may have given a boost to industrial productivity, but the boom has not created enough jobs. India's performance on this front has fallen short of target in the past. India's labour force is growing at a rate of 2.5 per cent, but employment is growing only at 2.3 per cent. The country is faced with the challenge of not only absorbing new entrants in the job market (estimated at seven million people every year), but also clearing the backlog. Unemployed youth is likely to translate his frustration into criminal and illegal activities.

Poverty Concerns

Poverty as measured by the new international Multi-dimensional Poverty Index (MPI), about 645 million people or 55 per cent of our country's population is poor as measured by composite indicator made up of ten markers of education, health and standard living achievements levels. MPI attempts to capture more than just income poverty at household level.

It is comprised of ten indicators: years of schooling and child education; child mortality and nutrition (health); and electricity, flooring, drinking water, sanitation, cooking fuel and other assets. This may be a gimmick of the Western Countries to project themselves as superior to other developing countries, but certainly the indicators denote quality of life of the citizen of a nation. India needs faster pace of growth to achieve these standards for its teaming millions who are yet untouched by the Country's economic renaissance. India's number of millionaires grew by 51 per cent to 126700 in 2009 according to Merill Lynch and consultants Capgemini, boosted by buoyant economy which grew 8.6 per cent in the last fiscal quarter. But increasing wealth has not trickled down to the common man. Newly built multi-storeyed buildings symbolising India's growing economic power stand in contrast close to the slums presenting a pathetic picture of inequality. Poverty eradication still seems far away.

Literacy Issue

Literacy in India grew to 74.04 per cent in 2011 from 12 per cent at the end of British Rule in 1947. Although it is more than fivefold improvement, the level is well below the world average literacy rate of 84 per cent. India currently has the largest illiterate population of any nation on earth. India's literacy rate is increasing only sluggishly. Besides low literacy rate there is a wide gender disparity in the literacy rate.

Health Concerns

Great improvement has taken place in Public Health since independence, but the general health picture remains far from satisfactory. The Government is paying increasing attention to integrated health, maternity and child care in rural areas, but the efforts on health front needs to be intensified with spread of health awareness through education and mass movement.

Extensive Corruption

The licence raj in India from 1950s to 1980s sowed the seeds of corruption in the socio-economic structure of our country. Nexus between politicians and business community and criminals is known to all. In recent times criminalization of Indian politics has assumed alarming proportions. Some Parliamentarians face criminal charges, including human trafficking, embezzlement, rape and even murder. Candidates with criminal records win elections on the strength of their 'Bahubali' status. Paying to get a job done is a common phenomenon experienced by majority of our countrymen. In recent times food adulteration has stolen limelight in the News Channels, even fruits and vegetables are not left to grow normally, toxic injections are administered for their quick growth.

Tons and tons of synthetic milk and milk products are confiscated every other day by the Health Department officials but the perpetrators of these crimes who play with the health of unsuspecting masses are set free without any exemplary punishment. There is a parallel flourishing market of spurious in the country. Spurious medicines, beverages, cosmetics, food items all are sold without fear as greasing palm to get away is very easy. Scarcity may be the mother of corruption in general, but what do you say about politicians who have been found sleeping with currency notes under the mattresses and those who wear currency notes garlands made up of taxpayers' money and those who accept bribe for raising questions in the Parliament and those who openly accept bribe in the name of Party Fund. 'yatha Raja, tatha Praja'

Terrorism and Insurgency

India is faced with terrorism and insurgency both from across the border and from within. Partition of India and Pakistan was a parting gift from the British Empire before leaving the country forever. First it was large scale invasion by the 'Kabailis' in J&K, then widespread armed insurgency in Kashmir after disputed State elections in 1987. Terrorism and insurgency has left more than 53000 people dead till July 2009. Several militant groups backed by ISI of Pakistan are operating in Kashmir. Many a times the militants have targeted people in other cities and towns of the country in suicide attacks. Mumbai attack was an example of their immaculate planning and preparedness to terrorize the entire nation.

There has been proliferation of militant groups in recent times, with as many as 33 identified in J&K. Currently the country is facing most significant challenge from Islamist fundamentalist groups. If India is facing terrorist attacks from the militants trained from across the border, threat from the Naxalite groups within the country is no less. Maoists are killing people in several districts of the country.

Half hearted approach to tackle their insurgency and lack of political consensus on this issue has encouraged them to attack Paramilitary forces and common people at will. Unfortunately these Naxalite groups have tacit support of some politicians. With more and more successful attacks, the Maoists' menace has already grown big.

Competitor China

China which is India's competitor in becoming a superpower is empowering its youth by opening up high number of universities, imparting quality education and teaching English. India, on the other hand, is still fighting for implementation of quotas for students and faculty. Meanwhile, students with potential have to resort to continuing education in private universities which often fail to meet the required standards.

Gender Bias

Gender inequalities, female feticide and the treatment meted out to women in rural areas, child marriages, continuing practice of dowry and sati take away the leftover sheen from the Shining India. The major divide between the rich and the poor, lack of proper rural infrastructure even basic amenities like potable water, toilets, two meals a day, suggest that India has a long route to tread in becoming a superpower.

Upsurge of Regionalism

A strong wave of regionalism is threatening the Social fabric and democratic institution in the country. The Maharashtra Nav Nirman Sena (MNS), a Maharashtra based political party is operating on the motto of 'Bhumiputra' (son of the soil). Division of State population on the basis of birth and language is most unfortunate trend fraught with danger of disintegration and civil strife. If virus of this trend is transmitted to other States it will cause irreparable damage to 'unity in diversity'.

Social Security

According to a recent survey around 400 million persons in India are in the working age group, less than 7 per cent are in the organized sector and 93 per cent of the workers are unorganized. While organized sector workers have sufficient and reliable access to social security in the form of protection under the law against loss/ stoppage of income on account of illness, disability, old age, death, maternity, the unorganized sector which has been contributing more in GDP in the last five decades is deprived of sufficient and reliable access to promotional and protective social security. As the average number of the senior citizens increases the concerns about social security will become more pronounced.

Monsoon and Agriculture

Agriculture and allied sectors like forestry and village industry account for around 16 per cent of GDP and despite a steady decline of its share in GDP, is still the largest economic sector which plays a significant role in the overall socio-economic development of the country. Slow agriculture growth is a major area of concern as two-third of country's population depends on rural employment for living. Monsoon plays a crucial role in agriculture production. Due to lack of adequate irrigation system, increased dependence on monsoon has tremendous impact on Indian agriculture; failure of monsoon, as we have seen in the past, has the capacity to destabilize the entire economy of the country.

Any country on a growth trajectory has to face several hurdles created by external and internal factors during transition period. It largely depends on the collective will power of the citizens who face these challenges and overcome all obstacles that may come in the way of their country becoming a superpower. However, going by the slogan, *'man mai hai vishwas pura hai vishwas hum hongay kamyab aik din'*, we shall overcome someday.

Mahatma Gandhi

Mohandas Karamchand Gandhi, the magic man of Asia, an apostle of non-violence and preacher of truth, was born on October 2, 1869 at Porbandar (Gujarat). He belonged to a well-to-do family. He went to England to study Law and became a barrister. Then he returned to India and began to practice at the Bombay (Now Mumbai) High Court. But he was not much interested in the lawyer's profession.

He also went to South Africa. There he made efforts to improve the condition of Indians. He underwent numerous sufferings but remained steadfast in his convictions.

After returning from South Africa, Gandhiji jumped into the Indian politics. He could not bear the miserable Plight of the Indian masses suffering and starving under the British rule. Mahatma Gandhi sacrificed everything to uproot the British from the Indian soil.

Freedom was the breath of Gandhiji's life. In 1919, he started a non-violent and peaceful movement. Hindu- Muslim unity, removal of untouchability and use of Swadeshi goods were his lifelong missions.

Mahatma Gandhi was a man of sound and sterling character. In fact, he was a very noble soul. He wore a very simple dress and ate simple food. He was not merely a man of words but also of action. What he preached, he practiced. His approach to various problems was non-violent. He was a god-fearing person. He was the cynosure of all eyes. He was a friend to all and enemy of none. He was universally loved and liked.

The part played by Mahatma Gandhi on the stage of Indian politics is unforgettable. In those stormy days of the struggle for Indian independence, Gandhiji suffered and was imprisoned several times, but the freedom of the motherland remained his cherished goal. He guided the freedom fighters, launched the 'Quit India Movement' and was imprisoned again.

His entire life was a life of service and sacrifice, of devotion and dedication. This saintly statesman, thinker, writer and orator of India still shine like a star on the horizon of India politics.

His tragic death on January 30, 1948 plunged the entire nation into gloom. He was assassinated by Nathu Ram Godse. His death was the greatest blow to the force of peace and democracy. The memorable words of Lord Mountbatten are worth quoting "India, indeed the world, will not see the like of him perhaps for centuries." His death left a great vacuum in the life of the nation. The whole world still reveres and respects this wizard of the 20th century who has left an indelible mark on Time.